WHEN

GOD

CHOSE

MAN

Written by VICTOR A. CONSTIEN
Illustrated by ARTHUR KIRCHHOFF

CONCORDIA CATECHISM SERIES
Walter M. Wangerin, Editor

CONCORDIA CATECHISM SERIES

H 15

PRIMARY LEVEL God Loves You
God Makes Me His Child in Baptism
God Invites Me to Pray
God Gives Me His Law
God Made You Somebody Special
God Comes to Me in My Worship

ADVANCED LEVEL When God Chose Man
This Is the Christian Faith
And Live Under Him

Authorized by The Lutheran Church — Missouri Synod for development
by the Board of Parish Education, Arthur L. Miller, executive secretary,
guided by the catechism committee: Harry G. Coiner, Frederick Nohl,
Arnold C. Mueller, Waldemar W. Affeldt, Lewis C. Niemoeller.

Concordia Publishing House, St. Louis, Missouri
Concordia Publishing House Ltd., London, E. C. 1
© 1967 by Concordia Publishing House
Manufactured in the United States of America

Χαῖρε

This is a Greek word. We pronounce it ki're. It means "GREETINGS!" This may have been the first word which our Lord spoke to human beings after His resurrection. We read it in Matthew 28:9.

I use this word to greet you in the name of the living Lord Jesus Christ as you begin to study this catechism.

The greatest news in the whole world is in this catechism. It's all about God's grace and love in Jesus Christ. It tells about God's covenant with us in Holy Baptism. This is Book 1 of three catechisms.

Book 2 explains the teachings of the Christian faith as Dr. Martin Luther outlined them in his Small Catechism. Book 3 teaches about the worship life of the child of God, and the lessons follow the church year. I hope you get to study all three catechisms in our series.

A companion book to this catechism is the Pupil Guide. Your faithful use of this book will make the message of the catechism meaningful to you. Your teacher's copy of the catechism also includes many ideas to help you in the classes.

The lessons march right along the "time-line" which reaches from God's creation to today. You can see this "time-line" on the end pages of the catechism. There is also a little "time-line" at the head of each lesson from 5 to 56. Your teacher will explain the symbols. Look for the little drop of water which shows the place in time of the story of each lesson.

I hope you find this an exciting way of studying about God's work for our salvation. I pray that God's Holy Spirit will use this catechism with its Gospel message to enlighten you and keep you in the Christian faith forever.

Walter M. Wangerin, EDITOR

CONTENTS

WHEN GOD CHOSE MAN

SECTION ONE   GOD'S COVENANT WITH ME

1. WHEN GOD CHOSE ME

2. WHEN GOD BAPTIZED ME

3. WHEN GOD GAVE ME FAITH

4. WHEN GOD SPEAKS IN HIS WORD

1

WHEN GOD CHOSE ME

He bound Himself to me and
showed me who I am

GOD AT WORK

One day Jesus visited a tax office. He wanted to talk with a
friend who worked there. His name was Matthew.

Matthew was an Israelite. He worked for the Roman government. He collected tax money from his fellow citizens. Israel-

ites hated tax collectors because they made them think of their Roman rulers. The Israelites believed Matthew stole their tax money.

Jesus came to the tax office to ask this hated tax collector to be His disciple. "Follow Me!" He said. Matthew rose from his chair and left his job to follow Jesus.

Sometime later Matthew prepared a feast. He made Jesus the honored guest. He also invited some of his longtime friends. Many of these were tax collectors too.

When the Pharisees heard that Jesus chose a tax collector to be one of His followers, many of them objected. The Pharisees were proud of their holy lives. They thought they were too good to walk with such terrible sinners. Then when they saw Jesus at Matthew's dinner they asked the disciples, "Why does your Teacher eat with tax collectors and sinners?"

Jesus heard their question. He answered, "Those who are well do not need a physician, only those who are sick. You are too proud to know that you are sick. I came to call sinners to salvation."

A CLOSER LOOK

When Jesus chose Matthew to be a disciple, our Lord chose a man whom people hated. Jesus asked him to quit his job and follow God's call to service. He forgave Matthew his sin.

The Pharisees thought they could overcome sin by themselves. They looked down on tax collectors and other public sinners when they came to Jesus for forgiveness. Many Pharisees despised Jesus because He showed love to sinners.

Jesus brings God's forgiveness to sinners today. He wants all men to be His disciples. God leads sinners to know their evil and helplessness. He invites them to be His children. He forgives them and gives them new life.

11

TO HELP US REMEMBER

All men in this world are sinners as Matthew was. God tells us:

> There is not a righteous man on earth who does good and never sins.
>
> *Ecclesiastes 7:20*

All men are sinners even from the time of their birth.

>  Behold, I was brought forth in iniquity, and in sin did my mother conceive me.
>
> *Psalm 51:5*

But even though we are hopelessly lost in our sins, God in His mercy chooses us and calls us to be His own people. He does this in the words:

> Fear not, for I have redeemed you; I have called you by name, you are Mine.
>
> *Isaiah 43:1b*

Man's sin, like the pride of the Pharisees, leads only to death. But God's mercy for Jesus' sake calls sinners to forgiveness and to life. St. Paul summarizes this in these words:

> For the wages of sin is death, but the free gift of God is eternal life in Christ Jesus our Lord.
>
> *Romans 6:23*

WHAT THIS MEANS TO ME

I know that from the time of my birth I am a sinner. The Holy Spirit leads me to confess this. My sins are a heavy burden upon me. I face eternal death in hell.

But God in His love chose me. He loved me even before the world began. He sent Jesus to lift the burden of sin and rescue me. He calls me to follow Him in a life of service. I do not deserve this redeeming love.

God did not wait for me to come to Him by myself. I could not do that. He came and found me. He tells me that He is my God and I belong to Him. He calls me to His church. I can trust Him to keep me in His church until He finally calls me to be with Him in heaven.

MY PRAYER

Heavenly Father, give me an honest heart
so that I may make a sincere confession
of my sin. My evil thoughts, unkind words,
and disobedient ways have offended You.
But I pray that You will remember me
according to Your steadfast love and not
according to my sins. Thank You for
choosing me in Jesus to live in Your
kingdom and serve You.

AMEN.

Lord, 'tis not that I did choose Thee;
That, I know, could never be;
For this heart would still refuse Thee
Had Thy grace not chosen me.
Thou hast from the sin that stained me
Washed and cleansed and set me free
And unto this end ordained me,
That I ever live to Thee.

The Lutheran Hymnal 37, st. 1

2

WHEN GOD BAPTIZED ME

He made me a child
of the new people of God

GOD AT WORK

"Ananias," the Lord God said in a special vision to His servant.

"Here I am, Lord," Ananias answered.

"Get up and go to Straight Street. Ask at the house of Judas for a man from Tarsus by the name of Saul. At this moment he is praying. He knows that you will come in and lay your hands on him so that he may regain his sight."

Ananias was afraid of Saul. "I have often heard about this man," he said to the Lord. "He has done so much harm to Your people in Jerusalem. In fact he has authority from the chief priests to arrest anyone who prays to You."

"Forget about that and do what I tell you," the Lord said. "I have chosen this man to bring My name to many nations and to the people of Israel. I will show him what he must suffer for My name's sake."

Ananias left on his mission for the Lord. He found the house of Judas and was invited in to meet Saul. He laid his hands on him and said, "Brother Saul, the Lord Jesus has sent me so that you may regain your sight and be filled with the Holy Spirit. He is the same Lord Jesus who appeared to you on your way here to Damascus. He blinded you with His great light."

14

"You are to be a witness before the world," Ananias continued. "You must tell people everywhere what you have seen and heard. Now, why should we delay any longer? Rise and be baptized and wash away your sins, calling on His name."

Then Ananias baptized Saul, and God added him to His church as a new and powerful witness of God's grace. Saul became Paul, a missionary who testified boldly that Jesus is the Son of God.

A CLOSER LOOK

God baptized Saul and washed away his sins. He made Saul a member of His new community of believers. He gave him a new understanding of Christ's way. Through Saul God would keep adding other members to His church. He would give them the power to believe Saul's witness to the Savior who is the Lord of life.

Ananias explained that when God baptizes us He cleanses us. He said to Saul,

✠ Rise and be baptized and wash away your sins, calling on His name. *Acts 22:16*

What is Baptism?

Baptism is not water only, but it is water used together with God's Word and by His command.

What is this word?

In Matthew 28 our Lord Jesus Christ says: "Go therefore and make disciples of all nations, baptizing them in the name of the Father and of the Son and of the Holy Spirit."

What benefits does God give in Baptism?

In Baptism God forgives sin, delivers from death and the devil, and gives everlasting salvation to all who believe what He has promised.

What is God's promise?

In Mark 16 our Lord Jesus Christ says: "He who believes and is baptized will be saved; but he who does not believe will be condemned."

Luke writes in the Book of Acts that God added believers to His church through Holy Baptism. On the day of Pentecost after Peter's sermon,

Those who received his word were baptized, and there were added that day about three thousand souls. *Acts 2:41*

St. Paul says that by Baptism we are made a part of the body of Christ.

✠ For as many of you as were baptized into Christ have put on Christ. *Galatians 3:27*

WHAT THIS MEANS TO ME

When God baptized me He washed away my sins. He cleansed my heart so that Jesus may live in me and I in Him. Through faith in Him I have the strength to become a better servant of God.

God made me a child of His new people when He baptized me. He included me in the company of His own people. This is His covenant with me.

MY PRAYER

Thank You, gracious Father, for washing away my sins in Holy Baptism. Keep me in the company of believers. Help me and all believers tell others of Your power in this sacrament. In Your mercy let Your church grow as you add to its number those whom only You can save, in Jesus' name.

AMEN.

Baptized into Thy name most holy,
O Father, Son, and Holy Ghost,
I claim a place, though weak and
    lowly,
Among Thy seed, Thy chosen host.
Buried with Christ and dead to sin,
Thy Spirit now shall live within.

The Lutheran Hymnal 298, st. 1

3

WHEN GOD GAVE ME FAITH

He made Himself known to me
so that I can know Him

GOD AT WORK

"Go south," the angel of the Lord said to Philip. "Take the desert road which leads from Jerusalem to Gaza."

Philip set out. On his way he saw a man from Ethiopia. This man was a high official for his queen. He had been to Jerusalem to worship. Now he was in his chariot, returning home. He was reading.

God's Spirit said to Philip, "Catch up with the chariot." Philip ran up and heard the man reading from the Book of Isaiah in the Bible.

"Do you understand what you are reading?" Philip asked.

"No. I need help," he answered. He invited Philip to join him in the chariot. "Please tell me of whom the prophet is speaking here: himself or someone else?"

Philip told him what the prophet wrote. He told him that Isaiah was writing about Jesus.

As they were going along the road, they came to some water. "Look," said the Ethiopian, "here is water. Will you baptize me?"

He ordered the chariot to stop. Together he and Philip went into the water. Philip baptized him.

Then the Spirit of the Lord took Philip away. And the Ethiopian went on his way rejoicing.

A CLOSER LOOK

People cannot live in God's covenant until they know Him. But people cannot know Him until He reveals Himself. Through Jesus God makes Himself known to us. Jesus is God's Word in the flesh.

Philip told the Ethiopian how Jesus suffered for us according to God's promise. He told him also how God calls people to be His children through Baptism.

The Holy Spirit creates faith in us through the Gospel. This is the Good News that Jesus takes away the guilt of sin and conquers death for everyone. Faith is the trust that in the work of Jesus God is our Father. When we put our faith in Jesus we say "Yes" to all that God tells us about Himself in His Word.

TO HELP US REMEMBER

Paul reminds us that God the Holy Spirit puts faith in us through the power of His Word.

✠ Therefore I want you to understand that no one . . . can say ''Jesus is Lord'' except by the Holy Spirit.

1 Corinthians 12:3

So faith comes from what is heard, and what is heard comes by the preaching of Christ. *Romans 10:17*

In Luther's explanation to the *Third Article* we confess we owe everything to God.

I believe that I cannot by my own understanding or effort believe in Jesus Christ, my Lord, or come to Him. But the Holy Spirit has called me through the Gospel, enlightened me with His gifts, and sanctified and kept me in true faith. In the same way He calls, gathers, enlightens, and sanctifies the whole Christian church on earth, and keeps it united with Jesus Christ in the one true faith. In this Christian church day after day He fully forgives my sins and the sins of all believers.

WHAT THIS MEANS TO ME

Sin keeps me from knowing God. But God makes Himself known to me in Jesus. Every time I read or hear His Word He comes to me. His Holy Spirit makes me aware of His presence. He offers Himself to me. He puts faith in my heart so that I will trust and obey Him.

I am with God when He comes to me in His Word and I accept Jesus as the Lord of my life. He wants me to know Him well. I displease Him if I am satisfied to know so little about Him. God lovingly told me about Himself. In my love to God, I want to grow in understanding and doing His will.

MY PRAYER

Thank You, heavenly Father, for finding
me in the ignorance of my sin and
bringing me to Jesus and the truth.
Grant me grace to continue in the faith
to which Your Holy Spirit has called me.
Make me always ready to read, learn,
and remember Your Word so that my
faith in You may grow. Let Your Word
be taught to the joy of Your people
everywhere, through Jesus Christ, our
Lord.

AMEN.

O Holy Spirit, grant us grace
That we our Lord and Savior
In faith and fervent love embrace
And truly serve Him ever,
So that when death is drawing nigh,
We to His open wounds may fly
And find in them salvation.

The Lutheran Hymnal 293, st. 1

4

WHEN GOD SPEAKS IN HIS WORD

He reveals my place in His plan of salvation

GOD AT WORK

The apostle Paul traveled thousands of miles as a missionary for Christ. He told people everywhere the good news that Jesus rose from the dead. He taught that Jesus is the Son of God who forgives sins and sends God's Holy Spirit to all believers.

Paul had dangerous and exciting adventures on his trips. In the city of Lystra, his enemies stoned and beat him so badly that his friends thought he was dead. One of the friends who gathered about his limp body may have been a boy named Timothy. Perhaps they took Paul to Timothy's house where his mother Eunice and grandmother Lois nursed him back to health.

Paul knew that young Timothy could be a good minister of God. His mother and grandmother had been his faithful teachers of the Holy Scriptures all his life. Paul taught him how Jesus fulfilled all of God's promises in the Scriptures. He asked Timothy to come along with him on his missionary trips.

Many years later, Paul wrote a letter to Timothy. In this letter Paul reminded Timothy of his study of the Holy Scriptures and urged him:

"Continue in what you have learned from the Scriptures from your childhood on. These sacred writings teach you the way of salvation through faith in Jesus Christ. All Scripture is inspired by God. God gives His Scripture to us to teach us what we are to believe and how we are to live. Through the Scriptures, God makes a believer a complete person, able to do good works."

God blessed Timothy's work in the church.

A CLOSER LOOK

There were only a few believers in the city of Lystra when Paul made his first visit. But one of these was a boy who later became an important worker in Christ's church. This all began when his mother taught him the Holy Scriptures. Here God showed young Timothy His plan of salvation. From Paul he learned about God's new covenant in Jesus Christ. Later Timothy, as a pastor, taught these truths to many people.

God uses His sacred writings to reveal Himself and His blessed acts to us today. The Holy Scriptures, written by inspiration of God, tell us of His covenant of grace in Jesus Christ. Jesus commanded His disciples to teach His Word.

23

TO HELP US REMEMBER

Lois and Eunice helped Timothy to know God by teaching him from the Old Testament. Prophets wrote the Old Testament. Evangelists and apostles like Paul wrote the New Testament. God inspired them to write. Peter reminds us,

✠ No prophecy ever came by the impulse of man, but men moved by the Holy Spirit spoke from God.   *2 Peter 1:21*

In the *Third Commandment* God commands that we study His Word and obey it.

Remember the Sabbath Day, to keep it holy.

What does this mean for us?

We are to fear and love God so that we do not neglect His Word and the preaching of it, but regard it as holy and gladly hear and learn it.

God inspired His prophets to write these books of the Old Testament:

LAW	HISTORY	POETRY
Genesis	Joshua	Job
Exodus	Judges	Psalms
Leviticus	Ruth	Proverbs
Numbers	1, 2 Samuel	Ecclesiastes
Deuteronomy	1, 2 Kings	Song of Solomon
	1, 2 Chronicles	
	Ezra	
	Nehemiah	
	Esther	

MAJOR PROPHETS
Isaiah
Jeremiah
 Lamentations
Ezekiel
Daniel

MINOR PROPHETS	
Hosea	Nahum
Joel	Habakkuk
Amos	Zephaniah
Obadiah	Haggai
Jonah	Zechariah
Micah	Malachi

WHAT THIS MEANS TO ME

God speaks to me in the Holy Scriptures. Here He tells me of all that He has done to make me His child. He tells me about His covenant of grace in Jesus. He tells me that in my baptism He makes this covenant with me.

I thank God for bringing me to this class where I may meet God in His Word. As I begin these lessons, I pray that I may study and learn as Timothy did. I pray that I may be God's witness to others of His plan of salvation.

MY PRAYER

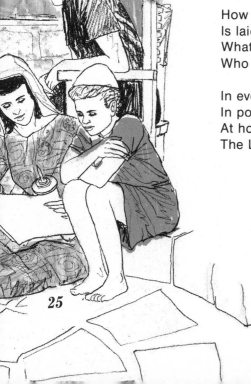

Lord Jesus, help me to know You as the Word of life sent from the Father. Help me to study and understand the Holy Scriptures which tell me what You have done for me. Thank You for Your Word, assuring me that You love me. Give me the power to do Your work.

AMEN.

How firm a foundation, ye saints of the Lord,
Is laid for your faith in His excellent Word!
What more can He say than to you He hath said
Who unto the Savior for refuge have fled?

In every condition, — in sickness, in health,
In poverty's vale, or abounding in wealth,
At home and abroad, on the land, on the sea, —
The Lord, the Almighty, thy strength e'er shall be.

The Lutheran Hymnal 427, st. 1, 2

5

WHEN GOD BEGAN CREATING

He made all things by the power of His Word

GOD AT WORK

In the beginning God created the heaven and the earth.

The earth was without form and empty. Darkness was everywhere. Only God was present. Out of nothing He made everything.

"Let there be light," God said. There was light. God saw that the light was good. He separated the light from darkness. God called the light day. He called the darkness night. The evening and the morning were the first day.

"Let there be a firmament in the midst of the water," God commanded. He called the firmament heaven. Then God called the dry land out from the waters and named it earth. He put plants and trees on the earth.

God put the sun, moon, and stars into the skies. "Let the waters bring forth swarms of living creatures," God ordered. "Let birds fly above the earth."

God made the animals that live on the earth and all the bugs and insects that creep along the ground and fly in the air.

When God created He simply said,

28

"Let there be." What He commanded came into being. He spoke and it was so. At first there was nothing. By His Word God made everything.

On the sixth day God said, "Let us make man in our image, after our likeness." So God created the first human beings. He made a man and a woman.

The seventh day was a different kind of day. On that day God rested. He made that day a holy, separate day. He gave the people whom He created time to worship Him.

When God saw everything He had made, it was all very good.

A CLOSER LOOK

What we see in the world shows us what our God is like. He is not only a powerful force, He is more. He is God, a personal God, wise and loving. He did not need the world. He created the world because He wanted to. This is God's love for us.

We have many questions about the beginning of the world. Some we will not be able to answer. We know only what God told us about it. That is why we go to our Bible. Here God speaks to us about Himself and His work.

When God made the world in six days and rested on the seventh, He gave people a pattern by which to live. We have days on which to work. We have a special day on which to worship God together. God gave us a day of rest so that we would have time and opportunity to worship Him in a special way.

TO HELP US REMEMBER

Praise God! By the power of His Word He created the beauty of the earth.

> By the Word of the Lord the heavens were made, and all their host by the breath of His mouth. *Psalm 33:6*

What we know about the world's beginning we know only by faith in the Creator. He told us about it.

> By faith we understand that the world was created by the Word of God, so that what is seen was made out of things which do not appear. *Hebrews 11:3*

In the *First Article* we bless the name of God, our Creator.

I believe in God the Father Almighty, Maker of heaven and earth.

What does this mean?

I believe that God has created me and all that exists. He has given me and still preserves my body and soul with all their powers. He provides me with food and clothing, home and family, daily work, and all I need from day to day. God also protects me in time of danger and guards me from every evil. All this He does out of fatherly and divine goodness and mercy, though I do not deserve it. Therefore I surely ought to thank and praise, serve and obey Him. This is most certainly true.

30

WHAT THIS MEANS TO ME

God is my Creator! His Word is powerful! His love is generous! I thank God for the beauty, color, and order of His world.

As God's child I can appreciate the wonders of His creation. Through the life and death of His Son Jesus He is my Father. I know that the world is His work. It is His world and I am His child in it. Wherever I look I know that I will see God's work.

The world continues by the Word of God. If He did not preserve it by His Word, it would fall back into nothing. I know that one day the world will end. On that day Jesus will come to take me and all believers to Himself in heaven.

MY PRAYER

O great Creator, thank You for Your wonderful works. Forgive me, for I have not always worshiped You. I have often made the things You created more important than You. Help me to know Your power and glory and love. Help me to be ready for Your coming.

AMEN.

We sing the almighty power of God,
Who bade the mountains rise,
Who spread the flowing seas abroad
And built the lofty skies.

On Thee each moment we depend;
If Thou withdraw, we die.
Oh, may we ne'er that God offend
Who is forever nigh!

The Lutheran Hymnal 43, st. 1, 6

6

WHEN GOD CREATED MAN

He put him in charge of creation

GOD AT WORK

When God made Adam and Eve He said, "Let us make man in our image, after our likeness. Let them have control over the fish of the sea, the birds of the air, the cattle, and everything else."

Genesis 1

So God created man. He formed man of dust from the ground. He breathed into man the breath of life. Man became a living being.

God put His man in the Garden of Eden. God told Adam that the fruits and vegetables were food for him and the animals. His job was to keep the garden growing.

Adam had no life partner. God said, "It is not good that the man should be alone. I will make a helper for him." Adam did not discover a helper among all the animals that he named.

So the Lord God caused a deep sleep to fall upon Adam. He took a rib from Adam while he slept and from it formed a woman. When he saw her, Adam said, "She shall be called woman, because she was taken out of man."

God blessed the first man and woman and said, "Be fruitful and have children. Fill the earth and work hard so that it may serve you."

After God had created Adam and Eve on the sixth day, He saw that everything which He had made was very good.

A CLOSER LOOK

God put man in the Garden of Eden to work. Adam was God's caretaker. His work kept up the garden.

God saw that Adam needed help. So God brought Eve to him. Together they would work in the garden and rule the earth for God. Together they would have children so that the earth might be filled. God made marriage when He brought Adam and Eve together as the first husband and wife, the first family. In marriage a man and woman leave their father and mother and live together as husband and wife under God's blessing.

God provided the way for Adam and Eve to have children. He placed a special power in the seed which both the father and mother have in their bodies. The seed of a father and mother meet in the mother's womb. When God blesses them, the power of the seed gives life to a new baby there. The baby continues to grow in the mother's womb and after a number of months it is born. This is how God continues His work of creation today. God's people thank Him for allowing them to work with Him in the creation of life.

TO HELP US REMEMBER

God gave Adam and Eve the blessing of sharing in creation.

God blessed them [Adam and Eve], and God said to them, "Be fruitful and multiply, and fill the earth and subdue it; and have dominion over the fish of the sea and over the birds of the air and over every living thing that moves upon the earth." *Genesis 1:28*

The Lord God said, "It is not good that the man should be alone; I will make him a helper fit for him." *Genesis 2:18*

In these words God created marriage and the family. Jesus talks about marriage in the following words.

✠ "'. . . a man shall leave his father and mother and be joined to his wife, and the two shall become one.' So they are no longer two but one. What therefore God has joined together, let no man put asunder." *Matthew 19:5-6*

God protects the family in the *Sixth Commandment.*

You shall not commit adultery.

What does this mean for us?

We are to fear and love God so that in matters of sex our words and conduct are pure and honorable, and husband and wife love and respect each other.

34

WHAT THIS MEANS TO ME

God wants me to help take care of His world. My work is to improve it. Then the world will become a better place to see God's power and wisdom. I must be careful about every living thing. I must not destroy what God has put into the world for man to use.

God has made me His own temple. God is alive within me through faith in Jesus. He gives me new power. He helps me think His thoughts, which are pure and holy. He helps me fight against the misuse of sex. He helps me speak with love and act with kindness toward my family and friends.

God promises forgiveness for my impure thoughts and unholy actions. In this forgiveness He gives me the power to put away my sins and live my life for Him.

MY PRAYER

Heavenly Father, You have created this world and made me one of its caretakers. You have put me in a family and given fathers and mothers the power to work with you to create new life. I praise You for Your gifts! Through Jesus' death, grant forgiveness for my evil thoughts and selfish desires. Make me strong to show my love for You by being respectful and loving to my family at all times.
AMEN.

Take my life and let it be
Consecrated, Lord, to Thee;
Take my moments and my days,
Let them flow in ceaseless praise.

Take my hands and let them move
At the impulse of Thy love;
Take my feet and let them be
Swift and beautiful for Thee.

Take my voice and let me sing
Always, only, for my King;
Take my lips and let them be
Filled with messages from Thee.

Take my love, my Lord, I pour
At Thy feet its treasure-store;
Take myself, and I will be
Ever, only, all, for Thee.

The Lutheran Hymnal 400, st. 1, 2, 3, 6

7

WHEN GOD BLESSED MAN

He wanted man to worship Him

GOD AT WORK

God made people different from everything else He made.

God simply spoke when He created the animals. He said, "Let the earth bring forth living creatures according to their kinds: cattle and creeping things and beasts."

And it was so. By the power of His Word God made them.

Then God decided to make a man. This time He said, "Let us make man in our image, after our likeness." God did not say this when He made the animals and plants. He said this only about the man and woman that He made.

So God created man in His own image. The Lord God formed man of the dust of the ground. God breathed into him the breath of life. This is how God began all human life. He breathed life into Adam and man became a living being.

God made man in His own likeness. He made man to know God. He made man holy so that he could talk to God and worship Him. Man had a likeness to God. The animals did not.

God talked to Adam and Eve about their life with Him. They spoke together about their work in the garden. They lived in happy communion with each other. Adam and Eve knew exactly what God wanted them to do. Because they were in His likeness they could do His will. They understood God's will and obeyed Him perfectly and cheerfully. They worshiped God with all their heart. They loved each other as God loved them. They helped each other remember what God is like.

What a wonderful life! God lived so close to them. They lived so close to God.

Genesis 1

A CLOSER LOOK

Animals received from God the kind of life He had already put into the world. But the life God gave to man was a different kind of life. God gave it to man alone.

God gave man his own kind of life so that He could speak with man directly. God made Adam and Eve so that they would listen to Him, think His thoughts, speak with Him, and obey Him.

God wanted people to live in close communion with Him because He had a special purpose for their lives. God made man to represent Him on earth. God made man and woman so that they could show each other what God is like. God is love. When people love one another as God loves them they show what God is like. This is people's most important work.

37

God took special care when He created the first man. He said:

> ✠ "Let us make man in our image, after our likeness." . . . So God created man in His own image, in the image of God He created him; male and female He created them.
>
> *Genesis 1:26-27*

Jesus Christ is the exact image of God. Through faith in Him God begins to restore the image which we lost when we sinned. Paul urges us:

> ✠ Be renewed in the spirit of your minds, and put on the new nature, created after the likeness of God in true righteousness and holiness. *Ephesians 4:23-24*

In Luther's explanation to the *First Article* we confess our faith that God has given us special gifts.

> I believe that God has created me and all that exists. He has given me and still preserves my body and soul with all their powers. He provides me with food and clothing, home and family, daily work, and all I need from day to day. God also protects me in time of danger and guards me from every evil. All this He does out of fatherly and divine goodness and mercy, though I do not deserve it. Therefore I surely ought to thank and praise, serve and obey Him. This is most certainly true.

WHAT THIS MEANS TO ME

God has given my life a high purpose. He has made me so that I can listen to Him, think His thoughts, speak with Him, and obey Him. He has made me so that I am able to show people what He is like.

The Holy Spirit has taught me that my sin spoiled God's plan for me. It ruined His image in me. But in Jesus God came to make me over into His image again. He gave me a knowledge of God's love and forgiveness. He turned my heart to God and put in me the desire to obey Him. God has promised to restore me to the full image of God. He will do this when He takes me to heaven by His grace.

I will try to show in my life what God is like so that others may trust His love and forgiveness too. When I serve others, God is working out His purpose in my life.

MY PRAYER

Heavenly Father, I am Your creation, the work of Your hands. But I have been unfaithful to Your plan for me. I have destroyed Your likeness. Yet You have loved and forgiven me. By Your Spirit You have begun to restore Your image in me. As I grow in my likeness to You let me show a greater love for my fellowman. In Jesus' name I ask it.

AMEN.

All people that on earth do dwell,
Sing to the Lord with cheerful voice.
Him serve with fear, His praise forthtell;
Come ye before Him and rejoice.

The Lord, ye know, is God indeed;
Without our aid He did us make.
We are His folk, He doth us feed,
And for His sheep He doth us take.

The Lutheran Hymnal 14, st. 1, 2

8

WHEN MAN MADE THE WRONG CHOICE

he tried to be like God

GOD AT WORK

Adam and Eve made a wrong choice. It all happened when the serpent tempted them.

"Did God say, 'You shall not eat of any tree of the garden?'" he asked. "Is it really true that God prevents you from eating of all the trees of the garden?"

"We may eat of the fruit of the trees of the garden," Eve answered, "but God said, 'You shall not eat of the fruit of the tree which is in the midst of the garden, neither shall you touch it, lest you die.'"

"You will not die," the serpent said. "God knows that when you eat of it, your eyes will be opened. You will be like God, knowing good and evil."

The serpent convinced Eve that the tree was good for food. The fruit looked especially delicious because she thought it would make them wise like God. She took some of the fruit and ate it. She also gave some to Adam, who was with her, and he ate it.

Then their eyes were opened. They knew that they were naked. They sewed fig leaves together and made clothes for themselves.

Toward evening, in the cool of the day, Adam and Eve heard the sound of God walking in the garden. They hid themselves from the presence of God. They stayed among the trees in the garden. They were afraid. Their choice of fruit had been rebellion against God. Now they knew how serious such rebellion is. Only God could make things come out all right again.

A CLOSER LOOK

In the Garden of Eden Adam and Eve had everything perfect. They could talk with God. He tested them with the choice among trees. They were to show that they were God's people by obeying Him. As they obeyed God their love for Him became stronger.

Then Satan used the snake for his evil ends. He convinced Eve that she was right in doubting God's love. Adam allowed himself to be tempted by Eve. Together they chose to follow their own wishes, as if they were God. They turned against God in pride and unbelief. They wanted to be God themselves, instead of letting God be God. This is the worst evil.

After they disobeyed God, Adam and Eve were afraid. Their eyes were opened, as the serpent said they would be. But what did they see? They saw their guilt before God. They had robbed themselves of perfect communion with God. Now they were under God's judgment.

TO HELP US REMEMBER

Satan wants us to think that our sins will help us to live. Jesus came to show that all Satan's words are lies.

✠ He who commits sin is of the devil; for the devil has sinned from the beginning. The reason the Son of God appeared was to destroy the works of the devil.   *1 John 3:8*

We share in Adam and Eve's wrong choice. All people are sinners.

✠ For there is no distinction; since all have sinned and fall short of the glory of God, they are justified by His grace as a gift, through the redemption which is in Christ Jesus.
                    Romans 3:22b-24

We are a creation of God. He alone is God. All creation is to worship and adore Him above all. That's what God means in His *First Commandment.*

You shall have no other gods.

What does this mean for us?

We are to fear, love, and trust God above anything else.

WHAT THIS MEANS TO ME

The story of the first man is the story of my life too. I can see that all men are sinful even before they actually commit sin. This sin separates man from God.

I am no better than Adam and Eve. I have tried to take God's place, too. I try to be equal with Him. This is the cause of misery and unhappiness in the world. This makes me unhappy too. When I am separated from God, I can only turn good to evil.

But God offers forgiveness to cancel my sin. In love He gave His Son Jesus to die for my sin. Through Jesus God brings me back again into communion with Himself. God continues to keep me in this communion through daily forgiveness. I can learn to love others as God loves me.

MY PRAYER

O God, when I disobey my parents or teacher, when I lie, when I show anger and hate toward schoolmates and friends, I am making the wrong choice even as Adam and Eve did. Forgive me all my sin. Give me Your Holy Spirit so that I can overcome Satan's temptations and honor You in my life. In Jesus' name.

AMEN.

My soul, now bless thy Maker!
Let all within me bless His name
Who maketh thee partaker
Of mercies more than thou darest claim.
Forget Him not whose meekness
Still bears with all thy sin,
Who healeth all thy weakness,
Renews thy life within;
Whose grace and care are endless
And saved thee through the past;
Who leaves no sufferer friendless,
But rights the wronged at last.

The Lutheran Hymnal 34, st. 1

9

WHEN GOD CURSED MAN

God promised the Second Adam

GOD AT WORK

"Where are you?" the Lord God called to Adam and Eve.

"I heard Your voice in the garden," Adam said. "I was afraid, because I was naked. I hid myself."

"Who told you that you were naked?" God asked him. "Did you eat of that tree I told you not to?"

"It was the woman's fault," Adam said. "She gave me some fruit from the tree and I ate it."

The Lord God said to the woman, "What have you done?"

"The serpent deceived me and I ate," she answered.

God said to the serpent, "Because you have done this you are cursed above all the animals. I will put enmity between

you and the woman, and between your seed and her Seed. He shall bruise your head, and you shall bruise His heel."

To the woman God said, "In pain you shall bring forth children. Yet your desire shall be for your husband. He shall rule over you."

God said to Adam, "Because you have listened to your wife and have eaten of the tree, the ground is cursed. It shall grow thorns and thistles. In the sweat of your face you shall eat bread. One day you will die and return to the dust of which you are made."

God put Adam and Eve out of the garden and guarded it so they could not return. Adam had to find a new place to work.

A CLOSER LOOK

God called Adam and Eve out of hiding. (No one can hide from God although sometimes people think they can.) He wanted them to repent of their sin and receive His forgiveness. Their sin had brought them under the curse of death. Death is separation. By our sins we deserve to be separated from God forever.

But even before God announced the curse of death for sin, He promised a remedy. The woman's Seed would crush Satan. Jesus is that promised Seed. He is the Second Adam who defeated Satan and united us with God again through forgiveness. Through Jesus' work of redemption God creates a new people to worship Him.

TO HELP US REMEMBER

God promised that the woman's Seed, the Second Adam, would break Satan's power. God said to Satan:

> ✠ "I will put enmity between you and the woman, and between your seed and her Seed; He shall bruise your head, and you shall bruise His heel." *Genesis 3:15*

Sin brought death to every person, Paul told the Christians at Rome:

> ✠ Sin came into the world through one man [Adam] and death through sin, and so death spread to all men because all men sinned. *Romans 5:12*

Jesus is the Second Adam, to reconcile us to God.

> ✠ For as by one man's disobedience many were made sinners, so by one man's obedience [Christ's] many will be made righteous. *Romans 5:19*

Martin Luther wrote: "God warns that He will punish all who break these commandments; therefore we are to fear His wrath and not disobey Him. But He promises grace and every blessing to all who keep these commandments. Therefore we are to love and trust Him and gladly do what He commands."

46

WHAT THIS MEANS TO ME

Sin is disobedience toward God. It is the strong voice in me that says No! to God's commands and will. Because I have sinned I face the curse of eternal death.

God has kept His promise to send the Second Adam. He is Jesus Christ, God's own Son. He brings forgiveness for my sin. He is my life with God, my Hope, and my Strength. He crushed Satan and freed me from the grip of death.

I serve God when I worship Jesus the Savior, sharing with others His free gift of eternal life.

MY PRAYER

> Heavenly Father, I cannot confess my sin
> unless You promise me Your mercy.
> Show me again the great love You have
> for me in Jesus. Turn my heart away from
> rebellion so that I am ready to receive
> Your forgiveness. Keep me in the
> faith which witnesses to Your love for all
> people in Jesus Christ.
>
> AMEN.

When sinners see their lost condition
And feel the pressing load of sin,
And Jesus cometh on His mission
To heal the sin-sick heart within,
All grief must flee before His grace,
And joy divine will take its place.

The Lutheran Hymnal 65, st. 1

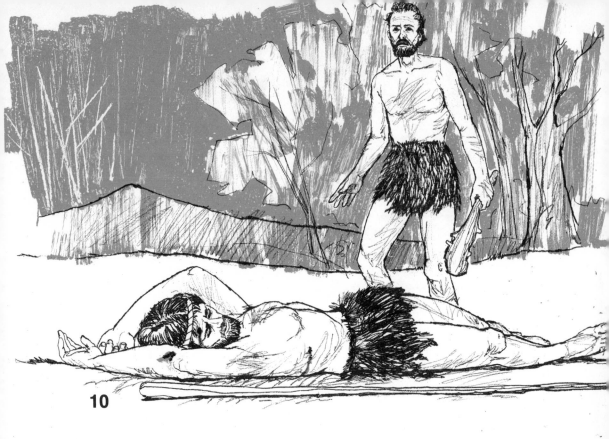

10

WHEN MAN HAD A SON

he was born in man's image

GOD AT WORK

Adam and Eve became parents. Eve gave birth to two sons, Cain and Abel. Cain grew up to be a farmer—and Abel a shepherd.

One day Cain brought some fruit from his garden as an offering to the Lord. Abel brought an offering too. He sacrificed some of his best sheep.

God was pleased with Abel and his offering. But He was not pleased with Cain. Cain became jealous of his brother and angry with God. God said to him, "If you do what is right, you will be accepted. But if you do not do right, sin waits at your door. It wants to rule you, but you must master it."

Cain did not listen to God. The jealousy in his heart grew. One day he killed his brother Abel.

A little later God said to Cain, "Where is your brother?"

"I don't know," Cain replied. "Am I my brother's keeper?"

"What have you done?" God asked. "The voice of your brother's blood cries to Me from the ground. The ground will not so easily grow food for you anymore. And you will be a run-away, a wanderer on the earth."

"My punishment is greater than I can bear," Cain cried. "Whoever finds me will kill me."

The Lord put a mark on Cain so that no one would kill him. Then Cain left the presence of God and lived in the land of Nod.

A CLOSER LOOK

Man's highest purpose is to adore God and obey Him. But Cain was born in sin. So the sin of jealousy turned him into a murderer.

Cain's heart was not right with God. That is why God did not accept his offering. Cain thought that if he went through the ceremony of an offering, that was enough. He did not thank God. He did not really feel the need for God's blessing.

Abel put his heart into his offering. He lived by faith in God's love for him. He depended on God's love to make his offering acceptable. He knew that God had given him everything he had. He wanted to stay under God's blessing. He said a true "thank you" to God by his offering.

49

TO HELP US REMEMBER

Micah tells us what God requires of us.

✠ "With what shall I come before the Lord, and bow myself before God on High?" . . . He has showed you, O man, what is good; and what does the Lord require of you but to do justice, and to love kindness, and to walk humbly with your God.   *Micah 6:6a, 8*

The *Third Commandment* reveals our need to worship God with fear and love.

Remember the Sabbath Day, to keep it holy.

What does this mean for us?

We are to fear and love God so that we do not neglect His Word and the preaching of it, but regard it as holy and gladly hear and learn it.

God wants us to show loving care for each other.

So then, as we have opportunity, let us do good to all men, and especially to those who are of the household of faith.
                    Galatians 6:10

The *Fifth Commandment* shows how God wants us to love our neighbor.

You shall not kill.

What does this mean for us?

We are to fear and love God so that we do not hurt our neighbor in any way, but help him in all his physical needs.

50

WHAT THIS MEANS TO ME

God accepts me as His child through His mercy in Jesus. He removes my sins and forgives them. Now I may come into God's presence with a happy heart. God accepts my worship for Jesus' sake.

When I don't care anymore what happens to my neighbor, I disobey God. But God has cancelled my sin so that I may help someone who is sick, lonely, injured, or in danger. I try to keep my heart free from jealousy. I try to say and do things which help instead of harm. I am more than my brother's keeper. I am my brother's brother.

God strengthens my faith when I study His Word and remember that He has made me His own in Holy Baptism; I can worship God only as He keeps me in the Christian faith.

MY PRAYER

Heavenly Father, accept my prayer and praise through Jesus Christ, Your Son. Cleanse me through His most precious blood. Help me put aside my selfish wants so that I will be good company for the lonely and a helper to the sick. Heal the injured, I pray, and protect any who are in danger.

AMEN.

Give me a faithful heart,
    Likeness to Thee,
That each departing day
    Henceforth may see
Some work of love begun,
Some deed of kindness done,
Some wanderer sought and
    won,
Something for Thee.

The Lutheran Hymnal 403, st. 3

51

11

WHEN GOD DESTROYED MAN

He saved Noah by His grace

GOD AT WORK

Adam's sons and daughters had children. Later these children also had children. Soon there were many people on the earth.

But the earth was no longer perfect, as God had created it. The people were born in Adam's image. They were all like him because they were sinful. The wickedness of sin grew and grew all over the world until God was sorry that He had made man. So the Lord said, "I will blot out man whom I have created from the face of the ground, man and beast and creeping things and birds of the air, for I am sorry that I have made them."

But God had mercy on one man and his family. His name was Noah. Before God destroyed wicked mankind, He ordered Noah to build a large boat or ark. God was planning to destroy men by a flood. The ark would protect Noah and his family from drowning. God commanded Noah to take two of each kind of animal and bird into the ark with him.

Then the Lord sent the Flood! It rained for 40 days and nights. Water poured up out of the land. Soon the water covered everything—even the peaks of the mountains. God judged His creation for its evil. All men and animals died in the Flood. But the ark floated safely on top of the flood waters, saving the eight people of Noah's family.

After a year and 10 days the waters receded and the boat was again on dry land. Noah showed that he believed in the mercy of God by thanking Him as soon as he stepped from the ark. He built an altar and offered sacrifices to the Lord.

God promised Noah that He would never destroy all men

this way again. He said, "I have set My bow in the cloud. It shall be a sign of My covenant with you and every living creature. The waters shall never again become a flood to destroy all flesh."

A CLOSER LOOK

When people do what they want to do and care nothing about God or His will, they can expect the judgment of God. When people turn away from God and refuse to be called back, they can expect Him to be angry. God will turn people over to their sins and let them go their way. The end is terrible punishment.

Man was created by God to do God's will. When man follows his own will, he has no God to be merciful to him.

Noah was not a perfect man, any more than we are perfect. He deserved punishment for his sin. But God loved Noah and rescued him. By saving Noah and his family, God shows us that He was still working His plan to save sinners. God revealed this love to all men in Jesus, His Son. Jesus is the great Rescuer. All who trust in Him receive the mercy of God and are forgiven.

53

TO HELP US REMEMBER

The *Law* reveals the wrath of God for all men. It tells us how we have failed to do His will.

The *Gospel* tells us what God has done and keeps on doing to save men. It is the message of God's grace through Christ. It is the power of God to save us; it creates in our hearts the faith to believe God's love.

God tells us that all men are sinful and under the judgment of His Law but that He will not destroy all men again:

> "I will never again curse the ground because of man, for the imagination of man's heart is evil from his youth; neither will I ever again destroy every living creature as I have done."
> *Genesis 8:21b*

> ✠ "I set My bow in the cloud, and it shall be a sign of the covenant between Me and the earth."
> *Genesis 9:13*

> ✠ Christ redeemed us from the curse of the Law, having become a curse for us.
> *Galatians 3:13a*

What does God say of all these commandments?

He says: "I, the Lord your God, am a jealous God, visiting the iniquity of the fathers upon the children to the third and fourth generation of those who hate Me, but showing steadfast love to thousands of those who love Me and keep My commandments."

What does this mean for us?

God warns that He will punish all who break these commandments; therefore we are to fear His wrath and not disobey Him. But He promises grace and every blessing to all who keep these commandments; therefore we are to love and trust Him, and gladly do what He commands.

WHAT THIS MEANS TO ME

God's Law shows me my sin. It judges me for not obeying God's commandments. It condemns me for my pride. It shows me the power and fearfulness of God's anger against sin. It drives me to Christ.

God's Gospel tells me that by His grace He rescued Noah from death. The Gospel shows me my loving Savior who lived and died and rose again to rescue me from death. By the water of Baptism and God's Word of promise I became His child forever.

I cannot explain this love of God which chose me for His family. Like Noah, I am amazed at my Lord's love which cares for me every day. I praise God for His grace.

MY PRAYER

Almighty God, Lord of heaven and earth, forgive my sins. I have thought too lightly of Your wrath. I have been slow to fear, love, and trust You above all else. Thank You for my Baptism. Thank You for rescuing me from eternal death. Help me to live as Your child in Jesus Christ.

AMEN.

The Law commands and makes us know
What duties to our God we owe;
But 'tis the Gospel must reveal
Where lies our strength to do His will.

The Law discovers guilt and sin
And shows how vile our hearts have been;
The Gospel only can express
Forgiving love and cleansing grace.

The Lutheran Hymnal 289, st. 1, 2

55

SECTION THREE   GOD'S COVENANT WITH ISRAEL

12

WHEN GOD CHOSE ABRAHAM

He made a covenant with Abraham

GOD AT WORK

The sons of Noah continued in the sinfulness of Adam. They did not honor God. They tried to make their own name more important than God's name. As punishment God scattered the people. In their new lands the people did not thank God for His mercy in saving Noah. They worshiped other gods. Did God give them another chance?

God had made a promise to Himself. He had said that He would send a Savior for all men. In that promise He tied Him-

self with love to His people. God kept His word. He chose a man by the name of Abraham to begin the carrying out of His promise.

Abraham's home was in Ur. Later he moved to Haran. God spoke to him so that he would know Him. He asked Abraham to trust Him as the God who promised to send the Savior. God also chose Abrahan to hear another promise.

"Leave your country and your relatives and your father's house. Go to the land I will show you," God said. "I will make of you a great nation. I will bless you and make your name great. You will be a blessing to people in every nation."

Abraham went where God told him. He came to the land of Canaan. There God appeared to him and said, "I will give this land to your descendants." Abraham believed God. He built an altar and worshiped God.

God knew that Abraham was often lonely and afraid. One night God called him out under the night sky. "Fear not, Abraham, I am your Shield," God said. "Look at the sky. Count the stars, if you can. That's how many descendants you will have." Abraham believed God.

God told Abraham and his wife Sarah that they would have a son, Isaac. As a sign of His covenant promise God told Abraham that every boy baby should be circumcised. Once again God showed that He loved even stubborn and sinful people.

A CLOSER LOOK

God found Abraham. Abraham did not find God by looking for Him in different places. Abraham did not climb up to God. God came down to Abraham. He took Abraham to Himself in love and forgiveness. Abraham had done nothing to make himself worthy of such high honor. Abraham, like the rest of his family, had very likely worshiped false gods. But in mercy God chose him. God made a covenant of grace with Abraham to send a Savior for all men.

God gave Abraham faith to believe these promises. So Abraham followed God into a new and strange country. Many times Abraham and Sarah were afraid and worried. They did not always trust God. But God always came to them with a new promise which would strengthen their love for Him. God wanted them to believe what He said and to follow where He led.

TO HELP US REMEMBER

God called Abraham to follow Him. With that call God created in Abraham the faith which obeys Him, and Abraham became a part of God's kingdom.

> By faith Abraham obeyed when he was called to go out to a place which he was to receive as an inheritance; and he went out, not knowing where he was to go.
>
> *Hebrews 11:8*

How are we a part of the covenant God made with Abraham? Paul wrote:

> Thus Abraham "believed God, and it was reckoned to him as righteousness." So you see that it is *men of faith* who are the sons of Abraham. *Galatians 3:6-7*

God calls us to repent and believe the Gospel. That's how we enter under His rule, into His kingdom. Once we do, we continue to pray in the words of the *Second Petition* that God's kingdom come to us and to others.

Thy kingdom come.

What does this mean?

God's kingdom comes indeed without our praying for it, but we ask in this prayer that it may come also to us.

When does this happen?

God's kingdom comes when our heavenly Father gives us His Holy Spirit, so that by His grace we believe His holy Word and live a godly life on earth now and in heaven forever.

WHAT THIS MEANS TO ME

God called me and made me His own in Holy Baptism. I deserved His anger because I sinned. Instead, in His mercy He chose me to receive eternal life. He adopted me into His covenant of grace. I am a member of His kingdom.

God plans to reach all men through the witness of His Word. I will keep on speaking of His plan and power. I will pray that the Gospel may come to men and women and children in my neighborhood and in all parts of the world.

MY PRAYER

> Heavenly Father, I have been weak and afraid. I have not always trusted You. Give me the kind of faith You gave Abraham so that I will follow where You lead me. Thank You for the grace which includes me in Your covenant of forgiveness. Extend Your kingdom so that people everywhere may live under Your grace through faith in Christ.
>
> AMEN.

My faithful God, Thou failest never,
Thy covenant surely will abide;
Oh, cast me not away forever
Should I transgress it on my side!
Though I have oft my soul defiled,
Do Thou forgive, restore, Thy child.

The Lutheran Hymnal 298, st. 4

13

WHEN GOD BLESSED JACOB

Isaac gave Jacob the covenant promise

GOD AT WORK

God tested Isaac and his wife Rebecca. He promised them a son, but He waited 20 years. Then He gave them two sons, twins. But only one of them would receive the blessing of being the father of God's own people. Which one would it be, Esau, the older, or Jacob, the younger?

When the boys grew up, Esau became a skillful hunter. He liked to be outdoors. He brought his father, Isaac, meat from his hunting. Isaac loved Esau more than Jacob. Jacob was a quiet man. He preferred to be at home. Rebecca loved Jacob more than Esau.

Rebecca wanted Jacob to receive the blessing from his father. But she knew that Isaac loved Esau more than Jacob. She was afraid that he would not give the blessing to Jacob. She planned a trick so that Isaac would bless Jacob. Since Isaac was old and almost blind, she dressed Jacob in Esau's clothes and put hairy skins on his arms. When Isaac touched him and ate the meat he brought, he thought Jacob was Esau. He gave him the special blessing.

Esau hated Jacob for taking this blessing away from him. He wanted to kill Jacob. Rebecca helped Jacob run away to her brother Laban's house. Before he left, Isaac said to Jacob, "God Almighty bless you and make you fruitful and multiply you. May He give the blessing of Abraham to you and your descendants. Then you will live in the land which God gave to your father Abraham."

Later, after Jacob was married and had sons of his own, he was able to make up with his brother Esau.

One evening, when he was on his way to Esau, Jacob had a visitor. God Himself came in the form of a man. Jacob wrestled with Him. Jacob said he would not let Him go until He had given Jacob a blessing. So God blessed him with a new name. It was Israel. That means: He strove with God. For God said: "You have striven with God and with men; you have prevailed." God treated Jacob as if he were a prince.

A CLOSER LOOK

Esau and Jacob were brothers, but they were also rivals. They both wanted the highest blessing from their father. Jacob, with the help of his mother, cheated Esau out of this blessing. That was not right; they lied. Where was God?

God was right there! He knows how selfish, jealous, and unfaithful people are. But He does not let man's sin ruin God's plans to save us. His blessing is always a gift of His grace. Men can never earn it. Neither did Jacob. It was in mercy that God chose Jacob to be the ancestor of the Savior. When Jacob trusted God, he was able to live in peace with his brother.

Because of his new name, the descendants of Jacob would be called "the Children of Israel." They were God's chosen people with whom He made His covenant of grace.

63

TO HELP US REMEMBER

God told Isaac and Rebecca about the sons He would give them. He said to Rebecca:

> "Two nations are in your womb, and two peoples, born of you, shall be divided; the one shall be stronger than the other, the elder shall serve the younger."
>
> *Genesis 25:23*

That prophecy came true when God gave the blessing to Jacob, the younger son.

After striving with Jacob, God gave him the blessing again.

> ✠ "Your name shall no more be called Jacob but Israel, for you have striven with God and with men, and have prevailed."
>
> *Genesis 32:28*

Jacob's 12 sons were the fathers of the Twelve Tribes of Israel.

God's grace chose Jacob to carry out His purposes. His mercy still calls people into His kingdom from all over the world. When Jesus commended the faith of the Roman centurion, He said:

> "Truly, I say to you, not even in Israel have I found such faith. I tell you, many will come from east and west and sit at table with Abraham, Isaac, and Jacob in the kingdom of heaven."
>
> *Matthew 8:10b-11*

64

WHAT THIS MEANS TO ME

I confess to God that I have been jealous. I have envied others for popularity, friendship, and success. Like Jacob I have tried to lie and deceive.

Yet God in His mercy has made me a member of His "new Israel," the Christian church. He gives me the privilege of striving with Him in prayer. I do this when I seek His blessing upon my petitions. When He blesses me it is always a gift of love. I have not deserved it.

I want to live in peace with others in my family, school, and neighborhood. I learn to do this as I learn to trust the God of Abraham, Isaac, and Jacob — who is also my God. He forgives my sins of envy and deceitfulness. By His grace I can carry out His purposes as one of God's "new Israel."

MY PRAYER

Gracious God and Father, I am not worthy of all the love and faithfulness which You have shown me in my life. Thank You for making me a member of the "new Israel," the church, by my Holy Baptism. Help me trust You and help me live in peace with others, for Jesus' sake.

AMEN.

Grace first contrived the way
To save rebellious man,
And all the steps that grace display
Which drew the wondrous plan.

Grace first inscribed my name
In God's eternal book;
'Twas grace that gave me to the Lamb,
Who all my sorrows took.

The Lutheran Hymnal 374, st. 2, 3

14

WHEN GOD CALLED MOSES

He announced the plan of the exodus

GOD AT WORK

The people of Israel were slaves of the ruler of Egypt. They had come to Egypt while Joseph was a governor. But now many years had passed and the Israelites had grown to a great number. Pharaoh became afraid that his Israelite slaves would become more powerful than their masters. He commanded his men to drown every baby boy born to the Israelites.

Exodus 1 — 3

But God had other plans for His people. He saw to it that one baby boy would not die at birth. Pharaoh's daughter found this baby in a basket at the edge of the river and wanted to claim him as her own. She named him Moses. He grew up in the palace of Pharaoh as a prince, but he never forgot that he was a member of the people of Israel. While defending one of his brothers, he killed an Egyptian man. Now he had to flee from Egypt. He went to the land of Midian where he did the work of a shepherd. God would now teach Moses how to be patient.

Many years went by. Israel was forced to do hard work for Pharaoh. Moses was still in the wilderness of Midian. It looked as though God had changed His mind about caring for His people. But finally God's time came. He said:

"I have seen all the trouble which My people have in the land of Egypt. I hear them crying for help. I want to free them from their slavery. I want to give them the land I promised to their fathers."

Then God called Moses. "I want you to lead My people out of Egypt to the land I have promised to them. You must go to Pharaoh and tell him to let My people go."

"But I can't do that," objected Moses. "I am no longer a prince of Egypt. I can't persuade Pharaoh to let the people go. I cannot speak well. They won't believe me. They will say that the Lord did not appear to me."

"I will go with you," God promised. "I will give you the power to do miracles. Your brother Aaron can speak for you. I, the Lord, will make you strong and wise. I will keep my covenant with Abraham, Isaac, and Jacob."

A CLOSER LOOK

The people of Israel enjoyed living in Egypt while Joseph was a ruler. But after many years went by, pharaohs ruled who

67

did not know Joseph. The Israelites had to do hard work. But God always knew of their trials and never forgot His covenant promises.

God called a special man to lead His people. God had prepared this man for his important work. Moses had received an education as an Egyptian prince; he had learned to be patient while out in the wilderness. God scolded him for wanting to refuse to be Israel's leader. But Moses learned to trust in the Lord for strength and wisdom.

God is faithful to all His promises. He carried out His great covenant promises with Israel through Moses. God keeps His promise to us today in our baptismal covenant. He has delivered us from slavery to sin, death, and the devil through the victory of our Savior, Jesus Christ.

TO HELP US REMEMBER

God's plan of exodus, by which He brought His people Israel out of their slavery in Egypt, was an act of His grace and love. This is how God announced His will:

> "I have seen the affliction of My people who are in Egypt, and have heard their cry because of their taskmasters; I know their sufferings, and I have come down to deliver them out of the hand of the Egyptians, and to bring them up out of that land to a good and broad land, a land flowing with milk and honey. . . . I will send you to Pharaoh that you may bring forth My people, the sons of Israel, out of Egypt."
> *Exodus 3:7-8, 10*

We praise God for His faithfulness to His covenant in the words of the psalmist:

> ✠ Rejoice in the Lord. . . . For the Word of the Lord is upright; and all His work is done in faithfulness.
> *Psalm 33:1a, 4*

The New Testament writer tells the story of Moses and shows how Moses believed in the promise of God:

> ✠ By faith Moses, when he was grown up, refused to be

called the son of Pharaoh's daughter, choosing rather to share ill treatment with the people of God than to enjoy the fleeting pleasures of sin. . . . By faith he left Egypt, not being afraid of the anger of the king; for he endured as seeing Him who is invisible. *Hebrews 11:24-25, 27*

WHAT THIS MEANS TO ME

I praise God for His faithfulness in His promises to Israel. He heard their prayers for help and answered them. I praise God for His faithfulness in His promises to me. He made me His own child in Baptism. He hears my prayers. He has redeemed me from the guilt and power of sin through the work of Jesus Christ.

But I still face trials in my life. God may use these to teach me to be humble and patient. He calls me to witness to His faithfulness. By faith I can show God's love in Christ to those who are about me in my life.

MY PRAYER

O faithful God and Father, You have graciously delivered Your people from their bondage according to Your promise. Give me the faith to see Your grace and love in my life. Especially when I am in difficulty strengthen my confidence in You. Help me to speak and live words of hope and love and forgiveness to many other people, for Jesus' sake.

AMEN.

The will of God is always best
And shall be done forever;
And they who trust in Him are blest,
He will forsake them never.
He helps indeed In time of need,
He chastens with forbearing;
They who depend on God, their Friend,
Shall not be left despairing.

The Lutheran Hymnal 517, st. 1

69

15

WHEN GOD TOLD MOSES HIS NAME

He made Moses His spokesman

GOD AT WORK

God spoke to Moses in a strange way.

One day as Moses was leading his flock to another pasture he saw a great sight. A bush was burning with a bright flame. Yet the bush did not burn up. "I must see what this is," Moses said to himself.

A voice called from the fire, "Moses!" And he answered, "Here I am."

"Do not come any closer. Take off your shoes. You are standing on holy ground. I am the God of your father, the God of Abraham, the God of Isaac, and the God of Jacob." Moses hid his face for he was afraid to look at God.

"I am come to deliver My people," God said. "I will send you to Pharaoh to bring the sons of Israel out of Egypt."

"What shall I say when they ask me who is sending me?"

"I AM WHO I AM. Tell them that I AM sent you. This is My name forever. They will listen to your voice. You and the elders of Israel shall go to the king of Egypt and tell him to let My people go." Moses went back to his father-in-law, Jethro, and told him what had happened. He said that he wanted to go back to Egypt to see his people.

Later God spoke to Moses again. "Tell Pharaoh, Thus says the Lord, Israel is My firstborn son. I say to you, let My son go that he may serve Me."

God told His people of His plan through Moses. Moses became a spokesman of the Lord to His people.

A CLOSER LOOK

When God told Moses His name, He revealed Himself to Moses. God's name is God Himself. God's name, I AM, means that God is the Creator of all life. God is Ruler over all people and all things. God never changes. He keeps all His promises. Moses would bring the word of the highest Ruler when he spoke to Pharaoh.

God made Moses His spokesman. Moses stood between Israel and the Lord. When the people sinned, Moses told them of God's judgment. Moses spoke God's Word of forgiveness, and he showed them God's faithfulness to His covenant with them.

71

When God sent His Son, Jesus, He sent the perfect Spokesman. Jesus is the Mediator between God and man. By His life, death, resurrection, Jesus speaks the Gospel of eternal salvation, of our rescue from sin and death, and of the faithfulness of God. He prays to God for us.

TO HELP US REMEMBER

Moses asked God:

"If I come to the people of Israel and say to them, 'The God of your fathers has sent me to you,' and they ask me, 'What is His name?' what shall I say to them?" God said to Moses, "I AM WHO I AM. . . . Say this to the people of Israel, 'I AM has sent me to you.'"

Exodus 3:13-14

God's name is holy, for it is God's revelation of Himself. He tells us this in the *Second Commandment.*

You shall not take the name of the Lord your God in vain.

What does this mean for us?

We are to fear and love God so that we do not use His name superstitiously, or use it to curse, swear, lie, or deceive, but call on Him in prayer, praise, and thanksgiving.

Through Jesus Christ, the perfect Spokesman and Mediator for God, God has freed us from the slavery of sin and death. Paul writes Timothy:

For there is one God, and there is one Mediator between God and men, the man Christ Jesus, who gave Himself as a ransom for all.

1 Timothy 2:5-6a

John writes about Jesus as Mediator:

If any one does sin, we have an advocate with the Father, Jesus Christ the Righteous; and He is the expiation for our sins, and not for ours only but also for the sins of the whole world.

1 John 2:1a-2

72

WHAT THIS MEANS TO ME

God's name makes God real to me. When I call on God's name I deal with God Himself. I want to use God's name with respect and awe. When I think how holy God's name is, I do not want to speak it uselessly or in anger.

I praise God that His name is "Savior." I really deserve His anger and punishment. But as Moses stood between God and Israel to tell the people of God's grace and mercy, so Jesus stands between God and me. Jesus is my Lord and Redeemer from all my sin.

God wants me to be His spokesman. He wants me to speak the Gospel to others. God wants all men to be saved. I pray that I may be a faithful spokesman for Him.

MY PRAYER

I praise You, O God, for being the same all the time. Thank You for revealing Your name to me. By Your Spirit, help me to give honor to Your name in my prayers and praise, through Jesus Christ, my Lord and Redeemer.

AMEN.

Father of glory, to Thy name
Immortal praise we give,
Who dost an act of grace proclaim
And bid us rebels live.

Immortal honor to the Son,
Who makes Thine anger cease;
Our lives He ransomed with His own
And died to make our peace.

To Thine almighty Spirit be
Immortal glory given,
Whose teachings bring us near to Thee
And train us up for heaven.

Let men with their united voice
Adore the eternal God
And spread His honors and their joys
Through nations far abroad.

The Lutheran Hymnal 248, st. 1, 2, 3, 4

16

WHEN GOD PROTECTED ISRAEL

He did it through the blood of the lamb

GOD AT WORK

God told Moses and Aaron to get ready for a night the children of Israel would never forget.

God told every family to kill a lamb that day. "It must be a male, a year old, without any defects," God said.

"Take some of the lamb's blood to the door of your house. Dip a twig of the hyssop plant into the blood. Then touch the sides and the top of the door with the blood."

"I will pass through Egypt that night," God said. "The oldest child in every Egyptian family will die. This is God's judgment on their sin. All their false gods must be destroyed. I only am the Lord God."

God explained His plans. "The blood on the doorposts will be a sign. When I see the blood I will pass over the house. The oldest child in your family will not die. I will pass over your families and you will be safe."

The Israelites ate the meat of the lamb at a special meal that night. Since they were getting ready to leave Egypt, they ate standing up. They were in a hurry to get away from Pharaoh. They wore their traveling clothes and sandals. In one hand they held a staff while they ate with the other.

At midnight many people in the land of Egypt died. Pharaoh's oldest child and the oldest child in all the Egyptian families died. Even the firstborn of the cattle died. This was God's judgment on the people of Egypt.

While it was still night, Pharaoh looked for Moses and Aaron. "Get out!—with all your people and your flocks and herds!" he

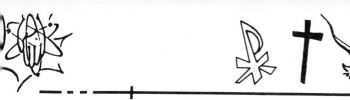

Exodus 12

said. So the people of Israel quickly left. God had kept His promise. The Israelites were free to go to the land which God had ready for them.

A CLOSER LOOK

In an act of great mercy God passed over the homes of the Israelites. He saved them from death. The Israelites would always remember this when they celebrated the Passover festival. They would tell their children what God had done.

God protected His people through the blood of the lamb of the Passover. The blood was God's sign to the people. When they saw it, they knew that God was faithful to His covenant with them. They would not be destroyed in Egypt. God had forgiven their sin.

75

God's perfect "pass over" is in His Son Jesus Christ. Because Jesus died for our sins, God in His mercy passes over our lives. He does not condemn us in our sins. For Jesus' sake He forgives our sins and cleanses us from all wickedness. This is the greatest act of God's mercy.

Jesus instituted the Lord's Supper to fulfill and replace the Passover meal. Under bread and wine Jesus gives His body and blood every time this Sacrament is celebrated. In His Supper He gives us His grace as we remember His sacrifice for us.

TO HELP US REMEMBER

When the people of Israel told their children about the feast of the Passover they said:

✠ It is the sacrifice of the Lord's passover, for He passed over the houses of the people of Israel in Egypt, when He slew the Egyptians but spared our houses.   *Exodus 12:27*

When Jesus instituted Holy Communion He gave unleavened bread and wine to His disciples to eat and to drink. He said, "This is My body and blood, given and shed for you for the remission of sins."

What benefits do we receive from this sacrament?
The benefits of this sacrament are pointed out by the words, *given and shed for you for the remission of sins.* These words assure us that in the sacrament we receive forgiveness of sins, life, and salvation. For where there is forgiveness of sins, there is also life and salvation.

WHAT THIS MEANS TO ME

God's great mercy in Jesus Christ has allowed me to escape His anger against my sin. If it were not for this "pass over," God's judgment on sin would declare me guilty. Like the people of Israel, I bow my head and worship Him who has showed me mercy.

When the Lord's Supper is celebrated in my congregation God assures me of His faithfulness to His people. He is still the covenant God who has promised to guard us against danger. I am kept by His power through faith unto salvation.

God spared me His judgment. He showed me His mercy. So I will show mercy toward my neighbor. God made me a member of His covenant people to strengthen me for service to Him. I serve Him when I help my neighbor know God's love for him. God is glorified when His mercy and love shine through me to my neighbor.

MY PRAYER

Gracious God, You separated Your people from the corrupt ways of Egypt. You delivered them so that they could serve You according to Your ways. I pray that You will help me see that You delivered me from the corrupt ways of the world. I beg the help of Your Spirit so that I do not receive your mercy in vain. Increase in me a merciful and forgiving spirit. Help people everywhere to receive Your grace in faith that they may be Yours in all eternity. Through Jesus Christ,

AMEN.

Praise the God of all creation;
Praise the Father's boundless love.
Praise the Lamb, our Expiation,
Priest and King enthroned above.
Praise the Spirit of salvation,
Him by whom our spirits live.
Undivided adoration
To the great Jehovah give.

The Lutheran Hymnal 37, st. 3

17

WHEN GOD RESCUED ISRAEL

He revealed His mighty salvation

GOD AT WORK

At last the people of Israel were on their way to the Promised Land.

Moses led the long line of men, women, and children, with all their cattle and sheep. But God showed His presence. He set a huge cloud in the sky to guide them and shade them. At night this cloud became a glowing fire.

On the third day after leaving Egypt the Israelites saw dust clouds rising from the road. Someone was coming fast with horses and chariots. It was the evil king of Egypt and his army. He was sorry he had let the Israelites escape. He wanted to make them his slaves again.

The people were terrified when they saw the soldiers coming. They saw they could not escape in the other direction because of the sea and mountains.

Moses shouted, "Stand firm! See the salvation which God will work for you today. God will fight for you!" Moses knew that God would save His people.

God told Moses to stretch his hand out over the sea. With a strong east wind God drove the sea back so that it looked like a wall on the right hand and on the left. A dry path waited for the Israelites. They could walk on the bottom of the sea. God prevented the Egyptians from catching them. A cloud and the darkness of night protected the Israelites so that the Egyptians could not find them.

In the morning the people of Israel were safely on the other side. But the Egyptians had followed them and were then in the middle of the sea. Suddenly their horses could no longer pull the chariots. The wheels stuck to the axles. Now it was the Egyptians' turn to be frightened. They knew God was punishing them.

God told Moses to stretch out his hand over the sea again. This time the water returned to its place. The Egyptians were drowned. The Israelites saw nothing but the water of the sea again.

When they saw how God had saved them, Moses sang a song to God. "I will sing to the Lord, for He has triumphed gloriously and has become my salvation."

A CLOSER LOOK

God's rescue at the Red Sea was the great act of deliverance for His Old Testament people. They traced their whole history back to this event. God proved to them that He was a faithful Father. Moses led the people in praise to God for His mercy.

The Egyptians learned—too late—that you cannot make fun of God's wrath. God punishes all who refuse to obey Him.

By Baptism God rescues His New Testament people. The crossing of the Red Sea is a type of God's grace to us in Baptism. We praise Him for His mercy.

TO HELP US REMEMBER

The people of Israel cried out to God for help against their enemies. Moses said:

✠ "Fear not, stand firm, and see the salvation of the Lord, which He will work for you today; for the Egyptians whom you see today, you shall never see again. The Lord will fight for you, and you have only to be still."

Exodus 14:13-14

The apostle Paul looked back on the history of Israel and wrote:

I want you to know, brethren, that our fathers were all under the cloud, and all passed through the sea, and all were baptized into Moses in the cloud and in the sea, and all ate the same supernatural food and all drank the same supernatural drink. For they drank from the supernatural Rock which followed them, and the Rock was Christ.

1 Corinthians 10:1-4

A thankful people praised God for His deliverance:

✠ "I will sing to the Lord, for He has triumphed gloriously; the horse and his rider He has thrown into the sea. The Lord is my Strength and my Song, and He has become my Salvation."

Exodus 15:1b-2a

WHAT THIS MEANS TO ME

When God saved Israel at the Red Sea, He showed His mighty power. The people praised and thanked Him for saving them.

God's power comes into my life. In my baptism He rescued me from slavery to sin and Satan. He made me His child. I praise and thank Him for His mercy and salvation. Through the life, death, and resurrection of Jesus, God makes and keeps me His own. He strengthens me in my temptations. He guards me from all evil. When I die He will bring me into His glorious presence.

MY PRAYER

O almighty God, by whose power the whole world was created and is now kept, watch over me in my life. Forgive me for forgetting Your power and Your mercy. Forgive me for my disobedience. For Jesus' sake, help me live a life of thanks and praise to You.

AMEN.

Through all the changing scenes of life,
In trouble and in joy,
The praises of my God shall still
My heart and tongue employ.

Of His deliverance I will boast
Till all that are distrest
From my example comfort take
And charm their griefs to rest.

Oh, magnify the Lord with me,
With me exalt His name!
When in distress to Him I cried,
He to my rescue came.

Oh, make but trial of His love!
Experience will decide
How blest are they, and only they,
Who in His truth confide.

The Lutheran Hymnal 29, st. 1, 2, 3, 5

18

WHEN GOD MADE A
COVENANT WITH ISRAEL

He chose Israel as His "own people"

GOD AT WORK

God is a powerful King who loved the people of Israel.

After they passed through the Red Sea, God's people traveled on. God led them by the cloud. Three months after they had left Egypt, they came to a land which Moses knew very well. He had been a shepherd there. Rising into the sky ahead of them was Mount Sinai. When they came into its shadow, Moses told the people to make a camp there. They were going to stay awhile.

God asked Moses to come up the mountain. Moses went up. God talked with him and told him to remind the people of Israel that He was their God. He loved them. He was their Protector,

Lord, and Friend. They had grumbled and complained against God. God still wanted them for His people.

"You saw with your own eyes how I delivered you from the Egyptians," God told them through Moses. "A mother eagle flies under her young. While they are learning to fly she keeps them from falling to the ground. That's the kind of protection I have given you. I have brought you safely all the way to Mount Sinai so that you may know and trust Me better."

God asked Israel to obey His voice and be His covenant people. That is why He did so much for them. From all the people of the earth He chose them for His possession. "I have a right to choose anyone I want," God said. "The whole earth is mine. My love has chosen you. I will make of you a kingdom of priests. You will be a holy nation. I have set you aside for special purposes."

"We want to be Your covenant people," the Israelites replied; they were all agreed. They said they would always obey and worship God.

A CLOSER LOOK

The Israelites were not a large and powerful nation. They had nothing to offer God. They were not a perfect people who acted as God wanted them to. God simply set His love on them. It all started with His mercy. He separated them from all the other people of the earth to carry out His purposes. From their nation God would bring the Savior to all men on the earth.

God saved Israel from death in the Red Sea. He rescued them from defeat at the hand of the Egyptians. He chose them and made a covenant with them. As their King He made their lives noble. He helped them serve each other and the people of other nations. He made them a kingdom of priests.

83

TO HELP US REMEMBER

God told the people of Israel the basis of His covenant with them.

"You have seen what I did to the Egyptians, and how I bore you on eagles' wings and brought you to Myself. Now therefore, if you will obey My voice and keep My covenant, you shall be My own possession among all peoples; for all the earth is Mine, and you shall be to Me a kingdom of priests and a holy nation."
Exodus 19:4-6a

God bound Himself to Israel because He had mercy on them. Moses reminded them:

✠ "It was not because you were more in number than any other people that the Lord set His love upon you and chose you, for you were the fewest of all peoples; but it is because the Lord loves you, and is keeping the oath which He swore to your fathers."
Deuteronomy 7:7-8a

Peter tells us that God chose us as children so that we might declare His wonderful deeds. Our work as God's people is to show by what we do and say that God has saved all men through Jesus. By His life and death and resurrection Jesus brought us out of the darkness of sin and death into the light of eternal life.

✠ But you are a chosen race, a royal priesthood, a holy nation, God's own people, that you may declare the wonderful deeds of Him who called you out of darkness into His marvelous light.
1 Peter 2:9

WHAT THIS MEANS TO ME

In my baptism God chose me and bound Himself to me. His love chose me. I have nothing to offer God! I have been selfish and inconsiderate of others. I have failed to worship Him. I have disregarded His will. Nevertheless, God set me aside for Himself. Because His own Son lived and died for me, God treats me as a special treasure.

Since God has separated me from the world through faith in Jesus I will be faithful to Him. As a member of His covenant people I have become a priest to my neighbor. I am God's representative telling him the mighty deeds of God to save us.

God has carried me "on eagles' wings." I will trust His care. I will serve Him by listening to His voice in His Word and learning to follow His commandments.

MY PRAYER

You have called me by Your mercy, gracious
Father, that I may know You and trust you.
Forgive me for acting as if I still belonged to this
world which passes away. I belong to You who
abide forever. Thank You for Your daily care and
faithfulness toward me. Help me and all Your
people appreciate our priesthood so that we may
serve one another in Jesus' name.

AMEN.

By grace I'm saved, grace free and boundless;
My soul, believe and doubt it not.
Why stagger at this word of promise?
Hath Scripture ever falsehood taught?
Nay; then this word must true remain:
By grace thou, too, shalt heaven obtain.

By grace! None dare lay claim to merit;
Our works and conduct have no worth.
God in His love sent our Redeemer,
Christ Jesus, to this sinful earth;
His death did for our sins atone,
And we are saved by grace alone.

The Lutheran Hymnal 373, st. 1, 2

WHEN GOD BOUND HIMSELF TO ISRAEL

Israel bound themselves to God

GOD AT WORK

God came down to a mountain top!

What a frightening day that was for God's people. Moses had ordered the people to make careful preparations for this day. They were to build a fence around the bottom of the mountain so that no one would come near it. They were to wash their clothing. They were to think about God's presence.

The great day began with rolling thunder and blinding flashes of lightning. Mount Sinai was covered with a thick cloud. Then came the very loud blast of a trumpet which made all the people tremble. While Moses and the people were standing at the foot of the mountain, the whole mountain shivered as God touched it!

Did God come down to destroy the people? Did He want to frighten them by telling them they would have to die?

God came down to tell Israel that He wanted them to be His people. God's loud message was:

"I am the Lord your God, who brought you out of the land of Egypt, out of the house of bondage. If you will obey My voice and keep My covenant, you shall be to Me a kingdom of priests and a holy nation. You must love Me above all. You must love one another. I will show steadfast love to the thousands that love and obey Me."

The people trembled when they heard God's voice. Moses told them that God was showing them His holy will.

All the people answered together and said,

"All that the Lord has spoken we will do."

A CLOSER LOOK

God came down to the mountain to claim Israel as His own people. He made a covenant with them. He would protect and bless them. They were to love Him and keep His commandments.

The people promised to obey. In their obedience they bound themselves to God. God had stirred their hearts to a new trust in Him. His commandments would guide their lives.

TO HELP US REMEMBER

God, who gave His laws, is the saving God. He told His people:

> ✠ "I am the Lord your God, who brought you out of the land of Egypt, out of the house of bondage. You shall have no other gods before Me." *Exodus 20:2-3*

God used blood to seal His covenant with Israel.

> They said, "All that the Lord has spoken we will do, and we will be obedient." And Moses took the blood and threw it upon the people, and said, "Behold the blood of the covenant which the Lord has made with you in accordance with all these words." *Exodus 24:7b-8*

Jesus gave a good summary of all the commandments of God as He spoke the words of Deuteronomy 6:5:

> ✠ "You shall love the Lord your God with all your heart, and with all your soul, and with all your mind. This is the great and first commandment. And a second is like it, You shall love your neighbor as yourself." *Matthew 22:37-39*

The people of Israel did not keep their covenant with God. They disobeyed His commandments and deserved His anger. Nevertheless God saved all those who trusted His forgiveness. Peter reminded the early Christians that all believers are saved only by God's grace.

> "But we believe that we shall be saved through the grace of the Lord Jesus." *Acts 15:11a*

WHAT THIS MEANS TO ME

In His commandments I come face to face with God. He shows me that He has a total claim on my life. But I have often said No to the will of God. My sin is that I have put my will against His will. For this God's judgment of eternal death hangs over me.

God's good news for me is that Jesus, God's Son, took the judgment against me upon Himself. In the life and death and resurrection of Jesus, God made me free from the guilt and power of sin. In Baptism God worked in me the faith which trusts Jesus. I am God's redeemed child and an heir of heaven. I will cast out of my heart any gods which oppose Him. I will worship Him alone. I must learn how to give my neighbor a larger share of the love which God has given me through the mercy of Jesus.

MY PRAYER

> Almighty God, Giver of the Law, make me to see
> and regret my sin, my refusal to obey You.
> Through Jesus' blood and by Your mercy remove
> my sins from Your sight. Grant me the grace to
> put You first in my life. Create in my heart a
> larger love for my neighbor so that I may share
> with him all Your gifts to me.
>
> AMEN.

That man a godly life might live,
God did these Ten Commandments give
By His true servant Moses, high
Upon the Mount Sinai.
  Have mercy, Lord!

God these commandments gave therein
To show thee, child of man, thy sin
And make thee also well perceive
How man unto God should live.
  Have mercy, Lord!

> Help us, Lord Jesus Christ, for we
> A Mediator have in Thee.
> Our works cannot salvation gain;
> They merit but endless pain.
>   Have mercy, Lord!

The Lutheran Hymnal 287, st. 1, 11, 12

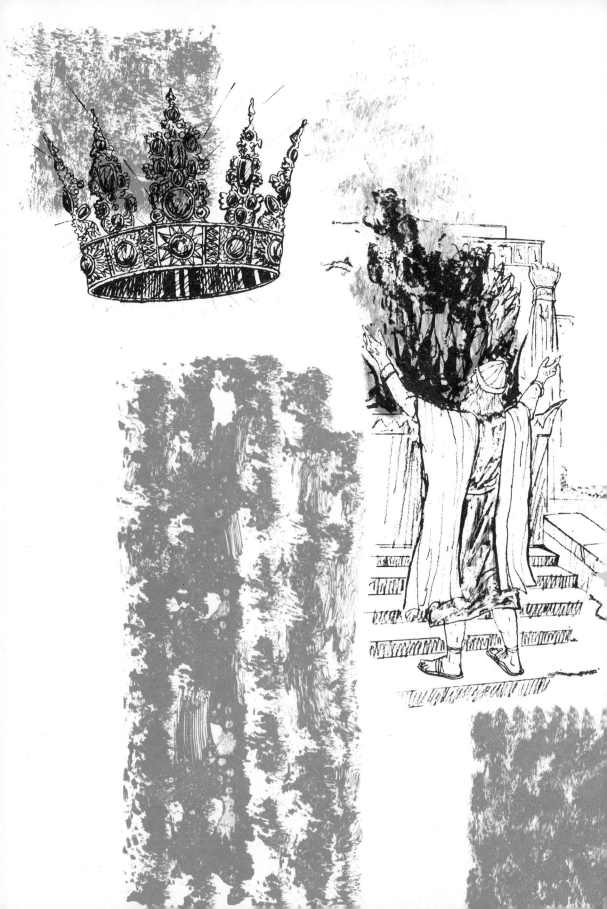

SECTION FOUR   GOD'S ACTIVITY IN ISRAEL, HIS OWN PEOPLE

20

WHEN GOD GAVE ISRAEL A LAND

He kept an old promise

GOD AT WORK

"All that the Lord has spoken we will do." This is what the people said at the foot of Mount Sinai. Not long after, Moses, at the Lord's command, sent 12 men to spy on the land of Canaan. When they returned, they showed the people the beautiful fruit which grew in the land. But they brought an evil report. They said that giants more numerous than Israel lived there. "We are not able to go against the people for they are stronger than we."

Then the people forgot their promise to the Lord. They rebelled against God saying, "Would that we had died in the land of Egypt! Or that we had died in this wilderness! Why does the Lord bring us into this land to fall by the sword?" Then they planned to choose a new leader who would take them back to Egypt.

God became angry at Israel's faithlessness. "I will strike them with sickness and death," He told Moses. Then Moses pleaded for the people. "I pray, pardon the sin of the people according to Your steadfast love, even as You have forgiven them since leaving Egypt." The Lord said, "I will forgive them, but none of these shall see the land I promised their fathers. They shall be shepherds in the wilderness for 40 years."

Forty years later, the Lord led the children of these people to the border of the Promised Land. Of the grown-ups only Joshua and Caleb were alive since that terrible day of rebellion against God. Moses died and Joshua was the new leader of Israel. He prepared the people for their entrance into the Promised Land.

"The priests will lead us as they carry the ark of the covenant of the Lord. Watch the ark and follow it. Prepare yourselves to see the great deeds of the Lord."

The march began. First came the priests carrying the ark of the covenant. As soon as they stepped into the Jordan River, the water stopped flowing. All of Israel crossed the river on dry land. Now the people were standing in the land which the Lord God had promised to their forefathers.

Joshua marked this great occasion by building a monument made of 12 stones which came from the middle of the Jordan River.

A CLOSER LOOK

In Lesson 12 we read the covenant promise which God made with Abraham: "I will give this land of Canaan to your descendants." God kept this promise and hundreds of years after this, the children of Israel entered the country. The 12 stones stood as a memorial to God's faithfulness to His promise.

93

Some of the Israelites doubted God. They complained to Moses and Aaron about God's ways. They wanted to rebel against the Lord and return to Egypt. God punished these people by delaying the time of Israel's entrance into Canaan.

God is the Giver of all our possessions today too. God will never break a promise He has made.

TO HELP US REMEMBER

The people of Israel could see the mighty acts of their covenant Lord. The land of Canaan was a gift from the Lord.

> ✠ You shall remember the Lord your God, for it is He who gives you power to get wealth; that He may confirm His covenant which He swore to your fathers, as at this day.
> *Deuteronomy 8:18*

Joshua's monument of 12 stones was to be a remembrance of God's great act.

> "When your children ask their fathers in time to come, 'What do these stones mean?' then you shall let your children know, 'Israel passed over this Jordan on dry ground.' . . . So that all the peoples of the earth may know that the hand of the Lord is mighty; that you may fear the Lord your God for ever." *Joshua 4:21-22, 24*

God, who is the Giver of all our possessions, tells us how to use these things. He protects these possessions by forbidding covetousness and stealing in the *Ninth Commandment.*

You shall not covet your neighbor's house.

What does this mean for us?

We are to fear and love God so that we do not desire to get our neighbor's possessions by scheming, or by pretending to have a right to them, but always help him keep what is his.

WHAT THIS MEANS TO ME

God has so many ways to show me that He loves me. By the simple water of my baptism He called me into His people. He gave me my parents who provide for my needs. They give me food, clothing, a place to live, protection, and love. I need never doubt that God is with me and for me.

But I do complain. There are times when I wish for something which someone else has. I begin to feel sorry for myself. I want to scold God for not answering my prayers. When I act this way, I am just like Israel when they wanted to go back into slavery.

God forgives me for my complaining and covetousness. For Jesus' sake He makes me able to show His love and faithfulness by my contentment and gratitude.

MY PRAYER

Heavenly Father, thank You for all Your wonderful gifts to me. Help me to see Your gracious presence in my life every day. By Your Holy Spirit, may I always have confidence in Your work of salvation through Jesus Christ, my Lord and Savior.

AMEN.

The Lord hath helped me hitherto
By His surpassing favor;
His mercies every morn were new,
His kindness did not waver.
God hitherto hath been my Guide,
Hath pleasures hitherto supplied,
And hitherto hath helped me.

Help me henceforth, O God of grace,
Help me on each occasion,
Help me in each and every place,
Help me through Jesus' Passion;
Help me in life and death, O God,
Help me through Jesus' dying blood;
Help me as Thou hast helped me!

95　　*The Lutheran Hymnal* 33, st. 1, 3

21

WHEN GOD CHOSE JUDGES

He cared for His people through men
like Gideon and Samuel

GOD AT WORK

God's people finally had a home. After they had lived in tents for nearly 40 years as they traveled from Egypt, God gave them their land. Joshua divided the land of Canaan so that each tribe had its own section.

But Israel's neighbors did not like them. From time to time they would band together to steal food and cattle from Israel. Sometimes they were so strong that they captured and made slaves of the Israelites.

The people often cried to God for help. God answered by reminding them that He had brought them out of Egypt and had given them their land. He had to punish the people for disobeying Him. But then God would choose a man to lead Israel to victory.

Once when the Midianites were the powerful enemies of Israel, the Lord called a man named Gideon. He was afraid to accept God's call. But God promised to help him He directed Gideon to choose only 300 men for his army. Each man was to carry a trumpet, an empty jar, and a torch. This small army was to battle against the thousands of men in the Midianite army.

Late one night Gideon quietly placed his men all around the camp of the sleeping Midianites. They had hidden their torches in the jars. At Gideon's signal, all 300 men dashed their jars to the ground, blew their trumpets, waved their torches, and shouted, "A sword for the Lord and for Gideon!" The sleepy

soldiers were terrified at the lights and the noise and in their confusion began to kill each other. Those that were not killed ran away thinking that they were fighting a powerful army.

Many years later God chose Samuel as a ruler of Israel. Already as a small boy, God used him as a spokesman. When Samuel became a man, he was a priest, a prophet, and a ruler of God's people. At this time the Philistines were Israel's powerful enemies. The people were afraid. Samuel told them:

"If you are returning to the Lord with all your heart, then put away the foreign gods from among you and direct your heart to the Lord and serve Him only and He will deliver you out of the hand of the Philistines." The people listened to Samuel and they put away their idols saying, "We have sinned against the Lord."

97

"I will pray to the Lord for you," Samuel promised. "Don't ever stop praying for us," the people asked. "Ask God to save us from the attack of the Philistines."

When Samuel brought his burnt offering to the Lord, the powerful Philistine army began to attack. But the Lord thundered with a mighty voice against them and threw them into confusion. Israel's armies won an easy victory with the help of the Lord. Samuel built a monument at this place to remember this victory. He called it "Ebenezer," which means: "The Lord has helped us."

A CLOSER LOOK

After Joshua died, Israel forgot God. The people forgot all that the Lord had done for them. He had freed them from slavery in Egypt and He had given them their own land. But the people worshiped Baal. God was angry at their idolatry. He punished them by letting their neighbors overpower them.

But when Israel cried out to God, He helped them. He was still their covenant Lord and He would not forget His promises even though the people sinned and forgot their promises. God's mercy moved Him to choose men to be "saviors" or "judges" of Israel. Each judge ruled the people only until the enemy had been conquered. Each judge was a direct spokesman of the Lord to Israel. Besides Gideon and Samuel, some of the better known judges were Deborah and Samson.

This is the way God was faithful to His covenant with Israel, His people.

TO HELP US REMEMBER

When Israel sinned, God punished them by letting their enemies become strong. When God had mercy on Israel, He chose judges to save them.

✠ Whenever the Lord raised up judges for them, the Lord was with the judge, and He saved them from the hand of their enemies all the days of the judge. *Judges 2:18a*

In Hebrews 11, the Bible's "Hall of Fame" chapter, these judges are mentioned as outstanding examples of faith.

And what more shall I say? For time would fail me to tell of Gideon, Barak, Samson, Jephthah, of David and Samuel and the prophets.

Hebrews 11:32-34

Samuel, the greatest of the judges, urged Israel to repent of their sins:

✠ "If you are returning to the Lord with all your heart, then put away the foreign gods . . . and direct your heart to the Lord, and serve Him only." *1 Samuel 7:3*

WHAT THIS MEANS TO ME

When God chose judges, He showed faithfulness to His covenant with Israel. I can learn from this that God never breaks His promises to His people. God made a covenant with me too. He promised to be my heavenly Father forever. My baptism is God's way of making this promise real to me.

Israel's judges can remind me of my perfect Savior. God gave His only-begotten Son, Jesus Christ, to be the Savior of the world. By His life, death, and resurrection, He makes me God's child, free from the power of sin, death, and the devil. By the power of His Holy Spirit, I can listen to God's voice in obedience, even as Samuel did when he was a boy.

MY PRAYER

Heavenly Father, I need Your mercy every day.
Make me bold and strong to serve You as Your
judges did long ago.   AMEN.

Seek where ye may To find a way
That leads to your salvation;
My heart is stilled, On Christ I build,
He is the one Foundation.

His Word is sure, His works endure;
He doth o'erthrow My every foe;
Through Him I more than conquer.

The Lutheran Hymnal 383, st. 1

22

WHEN GOD CHOSE DAVID

He anointed him king

GOD AT WORK

Many of the people of Israel wanted a king to rule over them. Others agreed with Samuel that they should not have a king. Finally Samuel listened to the people who wanted a king and made Saul their ruler. Saul was a tall, brave soldier. At first he ruled Israel well. Then he fell away from the Lord and became disobedient. God had to choose a new ruler.

One day God sent Samuel to Bethlehem to the house of Jesse. God had chosen one of Jesse's sons to be the king of Israel. Samuel was to anoint the new king. This would be an exciting event, for Jesse had many sons, and Samuel did not know whom the Lord had chosen.

"I wish to see each of your sons," Samuel told Jesse. So the oldest son stepped forward. He was strong and handsome. Samuel thought, "This must be the Lord's choice." But the Lord said, "Do not look on the outward appearance. I look into the heart. I have not chosen Eliab."

Then Jesse had his other sons walk before Samuel. Each time the Lord told Samuel, "I have not chosen this one." So Samuel announced, "The Lord has not chosen any of these seven sons. Are all your sons here?"

"The youngest is out in the fields tending the sheep."

"Send for him," directed Samuel. The boy came when he was called. His name was David. Samuel saw that he was a handsome young man too.

"Anoint him," said the Lord. "This is the new king."

Samuel took a horn of oil and poured it over David's head right before his father and his brothers. God's Spirit came upon David from this time on. God had mighty things for David to do.

A CLOSER LOOK

Not all of the people of Israel wanted a king. Some agreed with Samuel that this was not the way God wanted to rule them. But finally Samuel gave in to the people who did demand a king. God used this request of the people to provide a picture of the King who was to come someday. King David became the symbol of the kingship of Jesus Christ. The prophets of God would speak of the throne of David. The psalms would sing of his long dynasty. For God promised David that his house would last forever.

David made Israel into a great nation. He fought and won many battles against Israel's enemies. The Spirit of the Lord made David a great and mighty king.

His house would last forever because the Son of God would be born of his descendants. Jesus is the anointed One of God, the Christ, who completed the plan of salvation for all sinners. Through His work God keeps His covenant of life with us.

TO HELP US REMEMBER

When Samuel saw Jesse's oldest son, he thought God wanted him to be king. But God had other thoughts. He told Samuel:

> "Do not look on his appearance or on the height of his stature, because I have rejected him; for the Lord sees not as man sees; man looks on the outward appearance, but the Lord looks on the heart." *1 Samuel 16:7*

One of David's greatest victories came before he sat on the throne as king of Israel. It was against the giant warrior Goliath. This was because God's Spirit came upon him when Samuel anointed him king.

> Then Samuel took the horn of oil, and anointed him in the midst of his brothers; and the Spirit of the Lord came mightily upon David from that day forward.
> *1 Samuel 16:13a*

When the angel told Mary of the birth of Jesus, he said her son would be a great king of the dynasty of David.

> ✠ "And behold, you will conceive in your womb and bear a son, and you shall call His name Jesus. He will be great, and will be called the Son of the Most High; and the Lord God will give to Him the throne of His father David, and He will reign over the house of Jacob for ever; and of His kingdom there will be no end." *Luke 1:31-33*

102

WHAT THIS MEANS TO ME

The story of King David is an exciting way for me to see how God keeps His promises to His people. God made David great, especially by sending His Son Jesus into this world as a member of David's family. I praise God when I confess that Jesus Christ is my Lord and King.

My King rules me by His grace and love. He called me into His kingdom out of mercy. God gives me His Holy Spirit so that I may believe that I am in the kingdom of His Son. God's Spirit helps me live as a loyal subject.

MY PRAYER

> Praise and honor to the King of kings, my Lord and Savior! Thank You for bringing me into Your kingdom. Forgive me my sin in which I sometimes try to join the kingdom of the devil and the world. Give me the Holy Spirit, that I may be able to lead others into Your kingdom of glory.
>
> AMEN.

Hail to the Lord's Anointed,
Great David's greater Son!
Hail, in the time appointed,
His reign on earth begun!
He comes to break oppression,
To set the captive free,
To take away transgression,
And rule in equity.

O'er every foe victorious,
He on His throne shall rest,
From age to age more glorious
All blessing and all-blest.
The tide of time shall never
His covenant remove;
His name shall stand forever—
That name to us is Love.

The Lutheran Hymnal 59, st. 1, 6

23

WHEN GOD DESCENDED
UPON JERUSALEM

He blessed Solomon's temple

GOD AT WORK

King David chose the new king to succeed him. "Let Solomon ride in the style of a king," David commanded. "Blow the trumpet, and say, 'Long live King Solomon.' He shall sit on my throne."

David was a man of war. His son Solomon was a man of peace. David wished to build a temple for God's glory. However, God said that Solomon should build the temple while the nation was at peace.

Solomon made an agreement with Hiram, king of Tyre. "I am going to build a house for the name of the Lord my God," he said. "I want to have cedars from Lebanon in this house. Will you cut them down for me? None of us can cut timber like your people can."

Hiram agreed. His people made rafts out of the logs they cut. They floated them down the sea coast. Solomon paid for the work with wheat and oil. Hiram was Solomon's good friend. He had also been David's friend.

Finally, after 7 years, the temple was finished. Solomon called all the people together to dedicate it.

The priests carried the ark of the covenant into the temple. They put all the holy vessels in their proper place. When the priests came out again, they could not continue their service. A cloud filled the temple. The glory of the Lord filled the house of the Lord.

1 Kings 1, 6, 8

Solomon said, "I have built You a house. In this place You may dwell forever."

The people of Israel listened to Solomon's prayer. "O Lord, God of Israel, there is no God like You. You keep Your covenant and show steadfast love to Your servants. Let the word which you spoke to David be confirmed. Let Your promise of a king for Israel come true."

"The highest heaven cannot hold You," Solomon said to God. "Neither can this house which I have built. But You have said that Your name shall be there. Watch over everyone who comes to worship You. Listen to the prayers of Your people. Even when heaven is Your dwelling place, listen and forgive."

After sacrifices to God and a great feast, the people went home. They thanked God for all His goodness toward them.

A CLOSER LOOK

God was present in heaven and in the temple at the same time. He said He would dwell in the temple. He promised that He would be where His name was. He was as close to them as His name on their lips and in their hearts.

God was present in the temple to remind Israel of His covenant with David.

105

An everlasting King would someday sit on David's throne. He would be the Son [descendant] of David. God's covenant with David came true when Jesus lived and died and rose again. Through Jesus, God confirmed His covenant for all people everywhere. God is merciful to forgive and save everyone. When people trust God's mercy in Jesus they live with Him forever.

TO HELP US REMEMBER

David wanted to build a temple for God. But God told him "your son who shall be born to you shall build the house for My name." When he dedicated the temple, Solomon said:

> "Now the Lord has fulfilled His promise which He made; for I have risen in the place of David my father, and sit on the throne of Israel, as the Lord promised, and I have built the house for the name of the Lord, the God of Israel."
>
> *1 Kings 8:20*

In the *Third Commandment* God commands that we worship Him by giving attention to His Word.

Remember the Sabbath Day, to keep it holy.

What does this mean for us?

We are to fear and love God so that we do not neglect His Word and the preaching of it, but regard it as holy and gladly hear and learn it.

WHAT THIS MEANS TO ME

God's glory filled the temple. God's highest glory is in His Son Jesus Christ, who came so that I might live with God forever. God has given me the high privilege of knowing Jesus as my risen and living Savior. He is with me every day. He lives in me.

God comes to me through His Word and promises. He helps me understand the covenant He made with me in Baptism. I will be faithful to my faithful God! I will listen to His Word, believe it, and obey Him. I will make His presence known to others around me. By showing them love, I can help them see what God is like: God is love.

MY PRAYER

Ever-present God, Father, Son, and Holy Spirit, forgive my forgetfulness. Help me know Your love and forgiveness through Jesus. Keep my faith strong so that I may be a blessing to others as I speak of Your holy name for their salvation.

AMEN.

God Himself is present;
Let us now adore Him
And with awe appear before Him.
God is in His temple—
All within keep silence,
Prostrate lie with deepest reverence.
Him alone God we own,
Him, our God and Savior;
Praise His name forever.

God Himself is present;
Hear the harps resounding;
See the hosts the throne surrounding!
"Holy, holy, holy"—
Hear the hymn ascending,
Songs of saints and angels blending.
Bow Thine ear To us here:
Hear, O Christ, the praises
That Thy church now raises.

The Lutheran Hymnal 4, st. 1, 2

24

WHEN ISRAEL WORSHIPED IDOLS

God divided the kingdom

GOD AT WORK

Solomon was a famous king; he was known for his great wisdom. People came from far countries to ask him questions. He was a wealthy king. Many ships brought gold and precious stones and spices to his kingdom. He had treaties of peace with rulers of many other nations. He had built the beautiful temple for Israel, and God had come to put His name on this place.

But King Solomon's heart turned away from the Lord. All

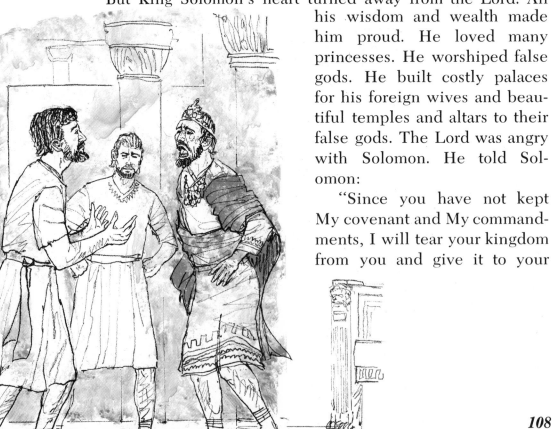

his wisdom and wealth made him proud. He loved many princesses. He worshiped false gods. He built costly palaces for his foreign wives and beautiful temples and altars to their false gods. The Lord was angry with Solomon. He told Solomon:

"Since you have not kept My covenant and My commandments, I will tear your kingdom from you and give it to your

servant. But for the sake of your father David, I will not do this in your days but in your son's days. For the sake of Jerusalem, I will give one tribe to your son."

This threat of God came true. After Solomon died, his son Rehoboam ruled in his place; but not for long. The people of the northern 10 tribes were tired of paying the high taxes for King Solomon's rich palaces and temples. They came to Rehoboam asking him to lower the taxes and lighten their work. Rehoboam consulted his counselors. Should he treat their request favorably? His younger advisers told him that he should be more strict than his father was.

Rehoboam took the advice of his younger nobles. "My father made your yoke heavy," he said harshly to the people from the North. "But I will add to your burden. If you do not obey, your punishment will be greater than ever!"

The people cried out against Rehoboam, "What part do we have any more with David and his kingdom? Go back home, Israel! Look after your own house, O Judah!" And with that they left the kingdom. David's proud nation was divided into two parts. Rehoboam, the grandson of David, was ruler only of Judah in the south, and Jeroboam was the new ruler of the 10 tribes to the north.

When the people of Israel had followed King Solomon into idolatry, God punished them by dividing their kingdom. It would never be a great kingdom again.

A CLOSER LOOK

When God made His covenant with Israel He had said, "I am the Lord your God. I am a jealous God. I will have no other gods before Me." As long as God's people worshiped and obeyed God they were blessed. But Solomon forgot the Lord. He put the gods of his foreign wives ahead of the Lord God of Israel. He led his people to rebel against the Lord. God punished Israel and the kingdom was divided.

Yet God's mercy remembered the promise to David and to the tribe of Judah. He kept His covenant with this remnant of Israel.

TO HELP US REMEMBER

Israel's idolatry and God's punishment upon them is an important example for us today. God demands to be first. This is the message of the *First Commandment*.

You shall have no other gods.

What does this mean for us?

We are to fear, love, and trust God above anything else.

I, the Lord your God, am a jealous God, visiting the iniquity of the fathers upon the children to the third and fourth generation of those who hate Me, but showing steadfast love to thousands of those who love Me and keep My commandments.

Martin Luther's explanation of this word of God speaks to us in our lives today:

God warns that He will punish all who break these commandments; therefore we are to fear His wrath and not disobey Him. But He promises grace and every blessing to all who keep these commandments; therefore we are to love and trust Him, and gladly do what He commands.

God proclaimed His love and mercy to Moses on Mount Sinai. This helps us explain His great patience with His disobedient people.

✠ "The Lord, the Lord, a God merciful and gracious, slow to anger, and abounding in steadfast love and faithfulness, keeping steadfast love for thousands, forgiving iniquity and transgression and sin." *Exodus 34:6-7a*

110

WHAT THIS MEANS TO ME

God is a just God. His Word of Law shows me my sin and guilt; I have made gods out of things in this world. In this way I disobey as Israel did.

But God's mercy moves Him to be patient with me. He has forgiven my sin. He keeps His covenant of grace with me. By His Spirit I can worship Him as the only true God and Jesus Christ as my Lord.

MY PRAYER

O God, forgive me my disobedience and idolatry. Help me see how great a sin it is when I put some person or thing ahead of You. Keep me in Your grace forever.

Jehovah, let me now adore Thee,
For where is there a God such, Lord,
  as Thou?
With songs I fain would come before
  Thee;
Oh, let Thy Holy Spirit teach me
  now
To praise Thee in His name through
  whom alone
Our songs can please Thee through
  Thy blessed Son!

O Father, draw me to my Savior
That Thy dear Son may draw me
  unto Thee;
Thy Spirit guide my whole behavior
And rule both sense and reason thus
  in me
That, Lord, Thy peace from me may
  ne'er depart,
But wake sweet melodies within my
  heart.

The Lutheran Hymnal 21, st. 1, 2

25

WHEN GOD'S PEOPLE CONTINUED TO SIN

God sent prophets to speak for Him

GOD AT WORK

Brave and faithful men spoke up for God.

God sent the prophet Elijah to tell King Ahab that a drought would wither the country of Israel. Ahab was very angry with Elijah. Ahab tried to kill him.

Then Elijah went away for 3 years. When Ahab saw him again, he greeted him: "Is it you, you troublemaker for Israel?"

Elijah defended himself. "I have not troubled Israel," he retorted, "you have! You have not obeyed God's commandments. You pray to the false god Baal."

Then Elijah called all the people of Israel to Mount Carmel. He proclaimed God's Word to them. "You are at the fork in the road. It is time for you to choose which way you will go. How long can you go without making up your mind? If the Lord is God, follow Him. If Baal is God, follow him."

What did the people answer Elijah? Not a word.

Elijah challenged them. "Let us prepare two sacrifices: each with an altar, the wood, and a bull's body. You call on your god and I will call on the Lord. The God who answers by fire, he is God."

The prophets of Baal prepared their sacrifice. "O Baal, hear us!" they begged. Nothing happened.

"Maybe he's asleep or busy," Elijah teased them. There was no fire, even though they cried to Baal all day long. They even cut themselves with knives to make Baal pity them.

Then it was Elijah's turn. "O Lord, God of Abraham, Isaac, and Israel, let it be known today that You are God in Israel."

Fire fell from heaven. It burned up the whole sacrifice, even the stones of the altar and the water which had been poured on it and which filled the trench around it. The people bowed and worshiped God. "The Lord, He is God," they said. God punished the prophets of Baal. He told Elijah to kill them.

A CLOSER LOOK

God gave His prophets a special knowledge of His will. He took hold of them with His Spirit. When God's people began to worship false gods, these prophets preached God's judgment against them. They worked to keep Israel faithful to the true God. They reminded the people of God's covenant of grace and mercy to forgive their sins.

A number of God's prophets wrote their messages. These are preserved as books of the Bible in the Old Testament. Habakkuk and Hosea are two of these prophets. Their books are the Word of God for us also today.

TO HELP US REMEMBER

When God sent Elijah to Israel, Elijah asked the people a sharp and important question:

"How long will you go limping with two different opinions?
If the Lord is God, follow Him; but if Baal, then follow him."
1 Kings 18:21

After God revealed Himself as Lord of all by burning Elijah's sacrifice, the people worshiped God saying:

✠ "The Lord, He is God; the Lord, He is God." *1 Kings 18:39b*

The prophet Hosea reminded Israel of their exodus as he told them of God's mercy. (This also refers to the infant Jesus' flight into Egypt, Matthew 2:15.)

✠ When Israel was a child, I loved him, and out of Egypt
I called my son. *Hosea 11:1*

God reveals Himself to us in His name. We worship God when we use His name in the right way. Jesus teaches us in the *First Petition* of His prayer to pray for the ability to worship God in what we say and how we live:

Hallowed be Thy name.

What does this mean?
God's name certainly is holy in itself, but we ask in this prayer that we may keep it holy.

When does this happen?
God's name is hallowed whenever His Word is taught in its truth and purity and we as children of God live in harmony with it. Help us to do this, heavenly Father!

WHAT THIS MEANS TO ME

God is great! He is the only God. He is angry when people give Him second place in their lives. Have I ever done this by fearing and loving someone more than God? Have I done this by disobeying all His commands to me?

God sends His prophets into my life too. My Christian parents, pastor, teacher, or one of my friends may remind me of my faithfulness to God and His Word. I am His child. Jesus lives in me by my baptism. This makes God first in my life.

MY PRAYER

Guide me, heavenly Father, in my life of service to You. Forgive me for trying to serve other gods. Help me make the right choices today and every day. Help me to show that Jesus lives within me in all that I say and do.

AMEN.

God of the prophets, bless the prophets' sons;
Elijah's mantle o'er Elisha cast.
Each age its solemn task may claim but once;
Make each one nobler, stronger, than the last.

The Lutheran Hymnal 483, st. 1

115

26

WHEN GOD PUNISHED ISRAEL

He destroyed Jerusalem

GOD AT WORK

God had to destroy a city to save His faithless people.

Some of the people of Israel were slaves in Babylon. Some remained in Jerusalem, their capital city. Wherever they were, many of them thought God would soon bring them all back to Jerusalem. The temple, the house of God, was there. As long as they had their temple, they thought, God would surely make them a strong nation again.

The people of Israel were trusting in their temple instead of in God. They were wrong in their hopes. God sent prophets to tell the people how wrong they were. He sent Jeremiah to Jerusalem and Ezekiel to Babylon.

"Maybe they will listen," God said to Jeremiah. "Maybe each one will turn from his evil ways. Then I will not punish them for their evil."

God gave Jeremiah a special announcement for the people. "Listen to Me. Walk in the Law which I have given you. Pay attention to the words of My prophets. If you don't, I will destroy the temple. I will make Jerusalem a city which all the nations despise. It will be ruined."

The people of Israel did not like Jeremiah's announcement. They did not like Jeremiah. They thought he was a traitor because he said Jerusalem would be destroyed. They did not listen to God's warning against their false worship and evil ways.

King Nebuchadnezzar of Babylon sent his army against Jerusalem. The warriors surrounded the city and battered the walls.

At last they broke through. They set fire to the king's palace.
They even destroyed the temple and tore down the city walls.
They took the people captive and led them away to Babylon as
slaves.

God made Jeremiah's words come true. God punished His
people because they had been unfaithful to Him.

117

A CLOSER LOOK

God was angry. Israel had turned the temple into an idol. They also worshiped their great city Jerusalem. This was idolatry. The people did not listen to God when He spoke through His prophets. They were not sorry for their sins and so they did not receive and trust God's mercy to forgive them.

Therefore God destroyed the temple and Jerusalem. He wanted His people to be sorry for their sins and turn to Him for help and forgiveness. God always helped His people in time of need or danger.

TO HELP US REMEMBER

Their false trust in the temple and Jerusalem deceived the people of Israel. God warned them against this. He urged them to repent and trust Him.

> ✠ "Thus says the Lord of hosts, the God of Israel, Amend your ways and your doings, and I will let you dwell in this place. Do not trust in these deceptive words: 'This is the temple of the Lord, the temple of the Lord, the temple of the Lord.'"
> *Jeremiah 7:3-4*

God's wrath destroyed Jerusalem because Israel was unfaithful.

> "And now, because you have done all these things, says the Lord, and when I spoke to you persistently you did not listen, and when I called you, you did not answer, therefore I will do to the house which is called by My name, and in which you trust, and to the place which I gave to you and to your fathers, as I did to Shiloh. Behold, My anger and My wrath will be poured out on this place, upon man and beast, upon the trees of the field and the fruit of the ground; it will burn and not be quenched."
> *Jeremiah 7:13-14, 20*

WHAT THIS MEANS TO ME

God destroyed Jerusalem. That shows me how important it is to take God's wrath against sin seriously. God's judgment of my sin makes me fear punishment for what I have done. It shows me that I can do nothing to please Him. My sin separates me from Him.

But I rejoice in the patience of God who always seeks my return to Him. In my baptism God has assured me that He is a "waiting Father." He is always eager for my homecoming through Jesus Christ, who died and rose again to return me to the Father's home.

This makes me thoughtful and sincere in my worship of God. I pay attention to His Word and ask His Spirit to lead me as I pray. I ask God to make my repentance sincere and my life an example of His love and mercy towards all men.

MY PRAYER

Take out of my heart every false pride, O God. Keep me humble, faithful, and honest as I speak to You and try to do Your will. Help me and everyone else to know the need for Your mercy and forgiveness in Jesus Christ. Let this be my hope of eternal life with You.

AMEN.

O'er Jerusalem Thou weepest
In compassion, dearest Lord.
Love divine, of love the deepest,
O'er Thine erring Israel poured,
Crieth out in bitter moan;
"O loved city, hadst thou known
This thy day of visitation,
Thou wouldst not reject salvation."

By the love Thy tears are telling,
O Thou Lamb for sinners slain,
Make my heart Thy temple dwelling,
Purged from every guilty stain.
Oh, forgive, forgive, my sin!
Cleanse me, cleanse me, Lord, within!
I am Thine since Thou hast sought me,
Since Thy precious blood hath bought me.

The Lutheran Hymnal 419, st. 1, 2

27

WHEN GOD SAVED THE REMNANT OF ISRAEL

He revealed the need for a suffering Savior

GOD AT WORK

God saw the deep need of His people for a Savior. As He punished their sin He wanted them to see their need too.

Nebuchadnezzar, king of Babylon, had destroyed the temple. Jerusalem was a rubbish heap. Once the Israelites had been a great nation. Now they were a poor, scattered people. But God rescued a faithful few. He called them "the remnant of Israel." They escaped His terrible judgment on Israel's idolatry. They trusted God to keep His promise of salvation. They were permitted to return to Jerusalem.

"I will make a new covenant with the house of Israel," God promised this remnant. "I will put My law within them. I will write it on their hearts. I will be their God and they shall be My people. They shall all know Me from the least to the greatest. I will forgive their iniquity. I will remember their sin no more." This was to take place through the coming Savior.

Jeremiah 31
Isaiah 53

The prophet Isaiah described the coming Savior as one who would willingly suffer and die for the people He loved:

"Like a lamb that is led to the slaughter, and like a sheep that before its shearers is dumb, so He opened not His mouth. . . . He poured out His soul to death, and was numbered with the transgressors. Yet He bore the sin of many. He made intercession for the transgressors."

A CLOSER LOOK

God watched over "the remnant" which He rescued. From this remnant He brought His Son Jesus, born of the Virgin Mary.

By the blood of Jesus shed on the cross God returns His people to Himself in mercy. This is His new covenant. God helps people serve Him from the heart through faith in Jesus.

God no longer requires ceremonies and church laws which people must learn and observe. He reveals Himself in Jesus. God will gather members from all nations into His church through their faith in Jesus.

TO HELP US REMEMBER

God promised His new covenant through Jeremiah.

 "I will put My law within them, and I will write it upon their hearts; and I will be their God, and they shall be My people. . . . I will forgive their iniquity, and I will remember their sin no more." *Jeremiah 31:33b, 34b*

God fulfilled His new covenant in His Son Jesus, foretold by Isaiah as the "Suffering Servant."

 He was despised and rejected by men; a man of sorrows, and acquainted with grief; . . . Surely He Has borne our griefs and carried our sorrows; . . . He was wounded for our transgressions, He was bruised for our iniquities; upon Him was the chastisement that made us whole, and with His stripes we are healed. *Isaiah 53:3a, 4a, 5*

WHAT THIS MEANS TO ME

If God had let Israel go their own way they would have destroyed themselves. Like Israel, I daily need the power of God to restore me. Through the forgiveness which Jesus brings, God changes my rebellion into obedience. His Spirit at work in my heart empowers me to walk in His commandments.

God has revealed Himself to me through Jesus, His Son. This shows His great love for me and all people. I know God Himself when I know Jesus who suffered and died for me.

God sometimes calls me to suffer for Him. When it is hard to do His will, He will help me.

MY PRAYER

O Holy Spirit, teach me my need for Jesus. Then let me take the full blessing of His forgiveness. Thank You for making Jesus known to me as the promised Savior, the fulfillment of God's covenant. Let Him be known to people everywhere as the world's Redeemer.

AMEN.

Behold, a Branch is growing
Of loveliest form and grace,
As prophets sung, foreknowing;
It springs from Jesse's race
And bears one little Flower
In midst of coldest winter,
At deepest midnight hour.

Isaiah hath foretold It
In words of promise sure,
And Mary's arms enfold It,
A virgin meek and pure.
Through God's eternal will
This Child to her is given
At midnight calm and still.

The Lutheran Hymnal 645, st. 1, 2

123

SECTION FIVE   GOD'S NEW COVENANT IN JESUS CHRIST

28

WHEN JESUS WAS BORN

God kept His promise for the Second Adam

GOD AT WORK

God sent the Second Adam.

God's first Adam sinned and died. Now *all* people deserve to die because all have sinned. All are children of this Adam.

In the Second Adam God makes people alive again. He gives eternal life through the sin's forgiveness which the Second Adam brings.

Jesus is God's Second Adam.

Matthew wrote how Jesus was born. Mary was engaged to Joseph. But before they were married the Holy Spirit worked a miracle in her. She conceived a son.

At first Joseph thought Mary had been unfaithful to him.

But an angel of the Lord appeared to him in a dream. "Joseph, son of David, do not be afraid to take Mary for your wife. That which is conceived in her is of the Holy Spirit. She will bear a son. You shall call His name Jesus, for He shall save His people from their sins."

Joseph now knew that God was keeping the promise He had made through the prophet Isaiah. "Behold a virgin shall conceive and bear a son," Isaiah had written. "His name shall be called Emmanuel." That means "God with us."

So the next day Joseph did what God had commanded. He took Mary as his wife. He treated her with love and understanding.

The time came for Jesus to be born. Mary and Joseph were visiting in Bethlehem when she brought forth her firstborn son. Because the city was crowded with other visitors, Mary could find only a manger in a stable for His bed. Into it she placed her son, the Savior of the world.

Later, when the apostle John thought about Jesus' birth, he wrote: "The Word became flesh and lived among us, full of grace and truth. We have seen His glory, the glory of the only Son of the Father."

A CLOSER LOOK

At last, God's hour came. At just the right time He sent His Son. Jesus came to redeem His people from the curse of God's law. Through faith in Jesus, God adopts us into His family as sons and daughters.

God kept His promise for a Savior through "the remnant of Israel." From the tribe of Judah, the family of Joseph and Mary, God preserved those who would be faithful to Him. His grace chose them to be the people through whom God would

127

bring Jesus into the world. This is His new covenant.

Jesus is God in the flesh. This is a wonderful mystery. God's love for His people is so great that He Himself came to be our Savior. He became the One who takes our sins away.

TO HELP US REMEMBER

Isaiah told God's promise of the coming Savior.

✠ For to us a Child is born, to us a Son is given; and the government will be upon His shoulder, and His name will be called "Wonderful Counselor, Mighty God, Everlasting Father, Prince of Peace." *Isaiah 9:6*

God named His Son Jesus. The angel told Joseph why.

"Joseph, son of David, do not fear to take Mary your wife, for that which is conceived in her is of the Holy Spirit; she will bear a son, and you shall call His name Jesus, for He will save His people from their sins." *Matthew 1:20b-21*

Jesus is God's eternal Word to us. Jesus is God for us forever.

✠ "In the beginning was the Word, and the Word was with God, and the Word was God. . . . And the Word became flesh and dwelt among us, full of grace and truth; we have beheld His glory, glory as of the only Son from the Father." *John 1:1, 14*

128

WHAT THIS MEANS TO ME

I am guilty of Adam's sin, too. I try to put myself into God's place as Adam did. I am only too eager to listen to the lies of Satan. I forget that I am God's creation, put on earth to serve and obey Him. I don't love God and my fellow human beings as God wants me to do. I have deserved to die for my sins against God.

When God sent the Second Adam He saved me. Through the forgiveness which Christ brings from His death on the cross, God gives me His kind of life. God chose me to receive this life because He is merciful. His mercy chose the remnant of Israel to bear His Son into the world. He has chosen me to bring the news of His Son's birth to the world. God was in Christ, reconciling the world to Himself.

MY PRAYER

Thank You, heavenly Father, for Your Second Adam, Jesus. Make me alive to Your purposes for me through faith in Him. Give me the courage to devote time, energy, and possessions to proclaiming the Good News: "Jesus saves His people from their sins."

AMEN.

But Christ, the Second Adam, came
To bear our sin and woe and shame,
To be our Life, our Light, our Way,
Our only Hope, our only Stay.

As by one man all mankind fell
And, born in sin, was doomed to hell,
So by one Man, who took our place,
We all received the gift of grace.

We thank Thee, Christ; new life is ours,
New light, new hope, new strength, new powers:
This grace our every way attend
Until we reach our journey's end!

The Lutheran Hymnal 369, st. 4, 5, 6

29

WHEN JESUS WAS BAPTIZED

God proclaimed His Sonship

GOD AT WORK

God announced to the whole world: "Jesus is My Son."

To prepare the way for Jesus, God sent John, the son of Zechariah. "Tell the people that the kingdom of God is close at hand," God told John. "Through your message I will turn them to Myself in repentance. Preach to them. Baptize them. Bring them My forgiveness. I will give them faith in Jesus."

Many people gathered to hear John teach. Some thought that he was the Savior. "No," said John. "The Savior is someone else who is much greater than I am. He is coming very soon."

One day Jesus came to John near the Jordan River. John knew Him right away! But he was surprised when Jesus said, "I am here for you to baptize Me."

"You should baptize me," John objected. "Why do You come to me?"

130

Matthew 3
John 1

"We must do it this way," Jesus answered. "This is part of God's plan to fulfill all righteousness." John agreed to baptize Jesus at that moment.

After the Baptism the heavens opened and God spoke. "This is my Son. I love Him. I am very pleased to choose Him for the work of saving people from sin."

As the Father spoke Jesus saw the Spirit of God come down from heaven like a dove. He rested on Jesus.

When people asked John about Jesus, John answered, "He is the Lamb of God who takes away the sin of the world. He is the Son of God. I baptize with water, but He baptizes with the Holy Spirit."

God opened the hearts of the people to listen to John and to Jesus. Some followed Jesus and became His disciples. They saw Jesus go all the way to the cross. They learned that by His death Jesus would bring eternal life with God to all who trust Him for it.

A CLOSER LOOK

When God spoke from heaven He told everyone that Jesus is more than a human being. God proclaimed that the man Jesus is His own Son — true God with the Father.

At His baptism God introduced Jesus to His ministry. With God's Spirit upon Him Jesus openly began His way to the cross. God the Father here calls Jesus His obedient Son. He did all things which God asks us to do. Everyone should listen to Him.

Jesus is perfect because He is God. He did not need Baptism for forgiveness. He never sinned. Jesus received Baptism to show how closely He tied Himself to the people for whom He came. He took our sin and was baptized for our forgiveness.

131

TO HELP US REMEMBER

When Jesus came from Galilee to the Jordan to John to be baptized by him, John tried to prevent Him, saying:

"I need to be baptized by You, and do You come to me?" But Jesus answered him, "Let it be so now; for thus it is fitting for us to fulfill all righteousness." Then he consented.
Matthew 3:14-15

✷ And when Jesus was baptized, He went up immediately from the water, and behold, the heavens were opened and He saw the Spirit of God descending like a dove, and alighting on Him; and lo, a voice from heaven, saying, "This is My beloved Son, with whom I am well pleased."
Matthew 3:16-17

✷ . . . he [John] saw Jesus coming toward him, and said, "Behold, the Lamb of God, who takes away the sin of the world! This is He of whom I said, 'After me comes a Man who ranks before me, for He was before me.' . . . And I have seen and have borne witness that this is the Son of God."
John 1:29-30, 34

WHAT THIS MEANS TO ME

Jesus entered His saving ministry for my sake! Could it actually be that He had me in mind when He began to teach and to suffer? Yes! That's the Good News of God's perfect plan. Jesus came to serve every sinner who needs God's forgiveness.

Jesus wanted to be baptized for my sake. He showed that He was ready to take my sins upon Himself. He offered to be the Savior. What Good News for me to share with my family and people everywhere! God's own Son has redeemed me.

MY PRAYER

Thank You, gracious Son of God, for obeying the Law. You received the Baptism which I need for forgiveness. You began and finished Your ministry so that I might be restored to Your Father and mine. You cleansed me from sin by Your death and resurrection. Increase my faith so that I may always hold to You as My only Savior.

AMEN.

When all the world was cursed
By Moses' condemnation,
Saint John the Baptist came
With words of consolation.
With true forerunner's zeal
The Greater One he named,
And Him, as yet unknown,
As Savior he proclaimed.

"Behold the Lamb of God
That bears the world's transgression,
Whose sacrifice removes
The Enemy's oppression.
Behold the Lamb of God,
Who beareth all our sin,
Who for our peace and joy
Will full atonement win."

Oh, grant, Thou Lord of Love,
That we receive, rejoicing,
The Word proclaimed by John,
Our true repentance voicing;
That gladly we may walk
Upon our Savior's way
Until we live with Him
In His eternal day.

The Lutheran Hymnal 272, st. 1, 3, 5

30

WHEN JESUS WAS TEMPTED

He revealed Himself as the new Conqueror

GOD AT WORK

God sent His Son to be the Conqueror over Satan and sin.

Jesus would fight God's battle against the devil until He won the victory. Now the time had come. The Holy Spirit led Jesus into the wilderness where Satan would tempt Him.

Jesus ate no food for 40 days and nights. He was hungry. "If You are the Son of God," Satan tempted, "tell these stones to become loaves of bread."

"But look what the Scriptures say," Jesus answered. "Man shall not live by bread alone. He lives by every word that proceeds from the mouth of God."

Satan took Jesus to Jerusalem and stood Him on the roof of the temple. "You are the Son of God," he said tempting Jesus the second time, "throw yourself down. The Scriptures say, 'He will give His angels charge of you.' The Scriptures also say, 'On their hands they will bear you up, lest you strike your foot against a stone.'"

Jesus corrected Satan. "The Scriptures also say, 'You shall not tempt the Lord your God.'"

For another temptation the devil took Jesus to a very high mountain. He showed Him the whole world. "I will give You all this," Satan said to Jesus, "if You will worship me."

"Get out of My presence, Satan!" Jesus commanded. "The Scriptures say, 'You shall worship the Lord your God. Serve only Him.'"

The devil left Jesus. Jesus had won this battle with him. Angels came to serve Jesus and worship Him. They showed again that Jesus is indeed God's Son. The Father sent them to strengthen Jesus for the work He had yet to do.

A CLOSER LOOK

Satan is always "the Tempter." He is a powerful enemy. He works to separate people from God. He tries to get people to

worship themselves or another false god. He deceives people by making them think he can give them special favors. The favors he promises are always lies.

Jesus conquered Satan. He resisted Satan's temptations. Satan could not deceive Him. Jesus proved that God is stronger than Satan and all evil.

Jesus' power to defeat Satan comes from His Father. The Father called Jesus His Son. Jesus is God's Conqueror for all of us. Through His victory we can conquer Satan too.

TO HELP US REMEMBER

Each time Jesus turned back the attack of Satan He quoted from the Holy Scriptures:

> "It is written, 'Man shall not live by bread alone, but by every word that proceeds from the mouth of God.'"
> *Matthew 4:4, quoted from Deuteronomy 8:3*

> "Again it is written, 'You shall not tempt the Lord your God.'"
> *Matthew 4:7, quoted from Deuteronomy 6:16*

> ✠ "Begone, Satan! for it is written, 'You shall worship the Lord your God and Him only shall you serve.'"
> *Matthew 4:10, alluding to Deuteronomy 6:13*

Because Jesus conquered Satan we can be confident that God will hear us when we pray:

And lead us not into temptation.

What does this mean?

God tempts no one to sin, but we ask in this prayer that God would watch over us and keep us so that the devil, the world, and our sinful self may not deceive us and draw us into false belief, despair, and other great and shameful sins. And we pray that even though we are so tempted we may still win the final victory.

136

WHAT THIS MEANS TO ME

Satan plots how he may come between God and me. He tries to make me believe that I am not God's child. He tempts me to doubt God and His love for me. My sinful self likes to team up with Satan to be contrary to God. Then I am also tempted to be selfish and unkind to people. I must recognize that quarrels, fighting, and discontent are the work of Satan.

Jesus conquered Satan for me. Through His victory I can resist Satan's temptations. The Father's promise to protect His children is for me, too. I will hold to His promise as I read God's Word. I pray God for the help I need to break Satan's attacks. I am confident that Jesus will keep me alert so that Satan cannot deceive me.

MY PRAYER

Gracious Father, deliver me from Satan and from every evil of body and soul. Keep me strong against every temptation to be disobedient or lazy. At my last hour take me from the troubles of this world to Yourself in heaven. For Jesus' sake.
AMEN.

Rise! To arms! With prayer employ you,
O Christians, lest the Foe destroy you,
For Satan has designed your fall.
Wield God's Word, a weapon glorious!
Against each foe you'll be victorious;
Our God will set you o'er them all.
Is Satan strong and fell?
Here is Immanuel. Sing hosanna!
The strong ones yield, With Christ our Shield,
And we as conquerors hold the field.

The Lutheran Hymnal 444, st. 1

137

31

WHEN JESUS SPOKE

He revealed God's kingdom to men

GOD AT WORK

A long time ago, God moved the prophet Isaiah to announce that the greatest Prophet was still to come. Isaiah said:

"The Spirit of the Lord is upon Me. He has anointed Me. He has sent Me to preach Good News to the poor, release for the prisoners, and recovery of sight for the blind." Of whom was Isaiah speaking?

Hundreds of years later a few worshipers in a synagog in Nazareth listened to a visiting teacher read these words of Isaiah. This speaker was Jesus of Nazareth. Most of the older people remembered when He was a boy playing in their streets.

Jesus finished the Scripture reading. He closed the book and in a quiet way preached a mighty sermon. He said:

"Today this Scripture has been fulfilled in your hearing." The people were listening to what the prophet Isaiah had promised! This time they heard this Scripture from the greatest Prophet Himself.

But they did not believe in Him. "Why don't You do miracles here as You did in Capernaum," they demanded. They thought if Jesus was so great He should bring honor to His hometown of Nazareth.

"No prophet is acceptable in his own country," Jesus replied. "Sometimes God's prophets perform a miracle for an outsider instead of God's people."

Then the people became so furious that they took Jesus to a high cliff just outside the town. They wanted to kill Him by throwing Him down to the rocks below. But Jesus simply walked away from them. No one could kill Jesus or even keep Him from His great work.

"I must preach the Good News of the kingdom of God to the other cities also; for I was sent for this purpose," was Jesus' way of describing the importance and scope of His work on earth.

A CLOSER LOOK

A prophet was a man who spoke in the place of God. God called certain men to be His spokesmen. Moses and Isaiah were prophets who spoke God's Word to the people. But Moses and Isaiah knew that God would send the greatest Prophet of all

139

after their time. It was this prophecy of Isaiah that the greatest Prophet, Jesus, read and fulfilled in the synagog in Nazareth.

Jesus spoke the Word of God. He is God speaking to men. Jesus preached the Good News, the Gospel of God's kingdom on earth. Jesus' Gospel calls people who are captives of sin and death to God's kingdom of forgiveness and life. God's kingdom is found among people who listen to Jesus and call Him their Lord and Savior.

TO HELP US REMEMBER

Jesus is the greatest Prophet of all. Moses told the people that God would send this great Prophet.

> ✠ "The Lord your God will raise up for you a Prophet like Me from among you, from your brethren — Him you shall heed."
> *Deuteronomy 18:15*

Simon Peter spoke of Jesus as the great Prophet to the crowd outside the temple. He quoted this word of Moses and then said,

> "God, having raised up His Servant, sent Him to you first, to bless you in turning every one of you from your wickedness."
> *Acts 3:26*

This was the reason for Jesus' insistent claim,

> ✠ "I must preach the Good News of the kingdom of God to the other cities also; for I was sent for this purpose."
> *Luke 4:43*

> ✠ "Repent, for the kingdom of heaven is at hand."
> *Matthew 4:17b*

WHAT THIS MEANS TO ME

I wish I could have been in Nazareth to hear Jesus read His own Bible passages. I can't believe that I would have wanted to hurt Him as the people tried to do.

Or would I? Jesus is the greatest Prophet today too. He speaks through my pastor, my Christian teachers, and my parents. When my mind wanders in church, when I dislike my studies, when I disobey my parents, I am turning my back on Jesus too.

Jesus is my Prophet. He is my Lord. By my baptism He called me into His kingdom. Thank God for Jesus' forgiveness! I praise Him for bringing me into His kingdom.

MY PRAYER

Thank You, Lord Jesus, for fulfilling God's promises. Thank You for coming into the world as the greatest Prophet. Thank You for bringing me into Your kingdom. Help me always to live as Your dear child.

AMEN.

Lord Jesus, who art come
A Teacher sent from heaven
And by both word and deed
God's truth to us hast given,
Thou wisely hast ordained
The holy ministry
That we, Thy flock, may know
The way to God through Thee.

Thou hast, O Lord, returned,
To God's right hand ascending;
Yet Thou art in the world,
Thy kingdom here extending.
Through preaching of Thy Word
In every land and clime
Thy people's faith is kept
Until the end of time.

The Lutheran Hymnal 485, st. 1, 2

32

WHEN JESUS PRAYED

He showed us how to pray

GOD AT WORK

Jesus often prayed to His heavenly Father. He wanted to obey His Father's will.

The disciples watched Jesus pray. One day as Jesus finished His prayers, a disciple asked, "Please teach us to pray."

"Do not be like the hypocrites when you pray," Jesus said. "They want everyone to see them and praise them for praying. So they make a show of their prayers in the synagog and on the streets. If they are looking for the praise of other people, that's the only reward they will get."

"Go to your room. Be all alone," Jesus continued. "Shut the door. Pray to your Father. He is there with you. He will answer your prayers."

"There is more. Do not babble on like the heathen. They think that many words will bring a better answer to their prayers. That's wrong. Do not copy them. Your Father knows what you need, even before you ask Him."

"When you pray, say:

Our Father who art in heaven,

Hallowed be Thy name.

Thy kingdom come. Thy will be done on earth as it is in heaven.

Give us this day our daily bread.

And forgive us our trespasses, as we forgive those who trespass against us.

And lead us not into temptation, but deliver us from evil."

(For Thine is the kingdom and the power and the glory forever and ever. Amen.)

Jesus wanted the disciples to know the right attitude with which to pray. He said to them, "If you forgive people their wrongs, your heavenly Father will forgive you. If you do not forgive people their wrongs, neither will your Father forgive your wrongs."

A CLOSER LOOK

Jesus taught His disciples to pray from the heart. A hypocrite only pretends to pray. Jesus warned His disciples not to be hypocrites.

Jesus revealed God as our all-knowing Father. God knows what we need better than we do. He knows how to bless us even before we ask Him. God answers our prayers because He loves us and is merciful. God wants to bless us.

143

Jesus gave His disciples the perfect model for all prayers. It's called the "Our Father," or "The Lord's Prayer." Jesus teaches us to pray for all our needs in the seven petitions of this prayer. There are spiritual needs as well as earthly needs.

TO HELP US REMEMBER

Jesus wants us to call God Father.

Our Father, who art in heaven.

What does this mean?

Here God encourages us to believe that He is truly our Father and we are His children. We therefore are to pray to Him with complete confidence just as children speak to their loving father.

Jesus invites us to pray with the confidence that our prayers will be answered.

✠ Verily, verily, I say unto you, Whatsoever ye shall ask the Father in My name, He will give it to you. *John 16:23*

We express this confidence in the word "Amen" which we speak at the close.

What does "Amen" mean?

Amen means *Yes, it shall be so.* We say *Amen* because we are certain that such petitions are pleasing to our Father in heaven and are heard by Him. For He Himself has commanded us to pray in this way and has promised to hear us.

WHAT THIS MEANS TO ME

The almighty God who created all things in this world is willing to listen to me when I talk to Him! Because of Jesus, I can call God Father. What a privilege this is for me!

There are so many things for me to ask. Sometimes I pray for the things I want rather than the things I need. Sometimes I pray as if I did not expect an answer to my prayer. Jesus taught me how to pray and what I should ask of God.

Every day I want to thank God in Christ for all His blessings to me.

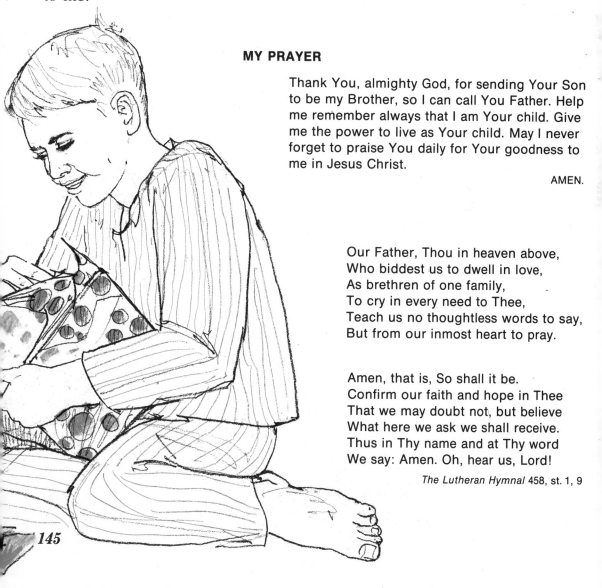

MY PRAYER

Thank You, almighty God, for sending Your Son to be my Brother, so I can call You Father. Help me remember always that I am Your child. Give me the power to live as Your child. May I never forget to praise You daily for Your goodness to me in Jesus Christ.

AMEN.

Our Father, Thou in heaven above,
Who biddest us to dwell in love,
As brethren of one family,
To cry in every need to Thee,
Teach us no thoughtless words to say,
But from our inmost heart to pray.

Amen, that is, So shall it be.
Confirm our faith and hope in Thee
That we may doubt not, but believe
What here we ask we shall receive.
Thus in Thy name and at Thy word
We say: Amen. Oh, hear us, Lord!

The Lutheran Hymnal 458, st. 1, 9

145

33

WHEN JESUS PERFORMED MIRACLES

He revealed that He is God's Son

GOD AT WORK

One day Jesus was invited with some of His disciples to a wedding in the city of Cana. Mary, Jesus' mother, was there, too. Everyone enjoyed the good food and wine which the host spread as a feast before the guests.

Then one of the servants noticed that they were running out of wine. Soon it would all be gone.

Mary knew the problem. She also knew the only one who could help. She quietly went to Jesus and said, "They have no wine." Jesus said, "My hour has not yet come." He would help—but later.

Some servants were working nearby. Mary asked them to be ready to do whatever Jesus said. They answered, "We will be ready."

John 2
Mark 2

A little later Jesus gave the servants an order. Jesus said, "Fill the water jars with water." They filled them to the brim. These water jars held 20 or 30 gallons each.

"Pour some out now and take it to the manager of the feast," Jesus said. The servants remembered their promise to Mary. They obeyed.

"This is good wine," the manager said, after he had drunk from the cup which the servants brought. He said to the bridegroom, "Most people serve the good wine first. When their guests have drunk freely they serve a poorer wine. You have kept the good wine until now."

At another time four men brought a friend who was paralyzed to Jesus. So many people were crowded around Jesus that they could not get close to Him. So the friends removed part of the roof where Jesus was teaching. They tied ropes to the mat on which their friend lay. They let him down in front of Jesus.

Jesus knew how unhappy the man was. He said to him, "Take heart, my son. Your sins are forgiven." First Jesus cured the man's sick heart. Then He cured his paralyzed body. He said, "Stand up. Pick up your bed. You can go home now by yourself." Immediately the man stood up, picked up his mat, and

147

walked out of the room. Everybody who saw this was amazed. They praised God. They said they had never seen anything like this.

A CLOSER LOOK

Jesus loved all people. He saw some who were hungry or sick. He wanted to help them. Sometimes He performed a miracle to feed them or to make them well. When Jesus performed miracles He revealed that He is God's Son.

Jesus looked for faith in those who saw His works of love. When people believed in Jesus as their Savior from sin they could see the greatness of His miracles. They could see how He was revealing Himself as the Redeemer sent from the heavenly Father.

TO HELP US REMEMBER

God's power continues. He still provides for our needs also through miracles of nature and history. When we pray the Lord's Prayer we depend on His power and His mercy. In the *Fourth Petition* we ask:

Give us this day our daily bread.

What does this mean?

God gives daily bread, even without our prayer, to all people, though sinful, but we ask in this prayer that He will help us to realize this and to receive our daily bread with thanks.

What is meant by "daily bread"?

Daily bread includes everything needed for this life, such as food and clothing, home and property, work and income, a devoted family, an orderly community, good government, favorable weather, peace and health, a good name, and true friends and neighbors.

WHAT THIS MEANS TO ME

The power with which Jesus forgave sins and cured the sick shows me that He is indeed the Son of God. He has revealed Himself as the promised Messiah, sent by God. The Holy Spirit recorded the miracles of Jesus in the Bible to increase my trust in Him as my Savior and Lord. Only as the Holy Spirit opens my eyes can I understand Jesus' miracles for what they really are.

My whole life depends on the power of God. He has given me life. He keeps me alive—body and soul. All I have comes from His creative hand. God's power is still active to create and maintain all things by His Word.

Often I need God's power in a special way. Sometimes the members of my family are sick. Many people throughout the world are hungry. God heals. God provides food.

MY PRAYER

> Gracious God, I thank You for Your love and care.
> If it is Your will give me health and strength to
> serve You. Watch over the sick and the suffering.
> Open my eyes of faith to see Jesus as my only
> Savior. Open my heart to help others for His sake.
> AMEN.

O God of Jacob, by whose hand
Thy people still are fed;
Who through this weary pilgrimage
Hast all our fathers led,

Our vows, our prayers, we now present
Before Thy throne of grace;
God of our fathers, be the God
Of their succeeding race.

Through each perplexing path of life
Our wandering footsteps guide;
Give us each day our daily bread
And raiment fit provide.

The Lutheran Hymnal 434, st. 1, 2, 3

34

WHEN JESUS RAISED THE DEAD

He showed that He is Lord of life

GOD AT WORK

Jesus is Lord of life. He begins life. He preserves life. He even restored life to someone who died.

One day Jesus came to the city of Capernaum. He had traveled by boat across the Sea of Galilee. When He landed a large crowd gathered around Him.

The head of one of the synagogs came up to Jesus. Jairus was his name. He fell on his knees at Jesus' feet. "My daughter is very sick. She may die any minute now," he said. "I beg You to come to my house. Lay Your hands on her. You can make her well. Then she will live." Jesus went with him to see the girl. She was about 12 years old.

But before they arrived at Jairus' house a messenger brought them sad news. "Your daughter is dead. We should not trouble Jesus any more."

Jesus acted as if He did not hear the sad news. "Don't be afraid," He said to Jairus. "Only have faith that I am able to help you."

Jesus told Peter, James, and John that they could come with Him. When they arrived at the girl's house they found people crying and moaning. Jesus asked them, "Why are you crying and moaning? The child is not dead. She is asleep." Then they laughed at Him.

Jesus asked everyone to step out of the room except His disciples and the girl's parents. He took her by the hand and said, "Get up, little girl." Immediately she opened her eyes, as if she were waking up from sleep. She got up and walked around. Her parents were amazed. Jesus reminded them to give her something to eat.

Mark 5
Luke 7

151

At another time Jesus went to a city called Nain. His disciples and a large crowd walked with Him toward the city gate. They met a funeral procession. The dead man was the only son of his mother, and she was a widow. Many people were with her.

When Jesus saw the sad mother, He felt sorry for her. He said, "Stop crying." He touched the board on which the dead son lay. The men who carried it stopped. "Young man, rise up!" Jesus commanded. The dead man sat up. He began to talk. Jesus gave him back to his mother.

Everyone who saw this honored Jesus and glorified God.

"A great prophet has come to us," they said. "God is visiting His people. God cares for His people."

A CLOSER LOOK

God made people to live. He never intended that they should die. But when Adam sinned he brought death into the world. Now all people must die because all people sin. When we think of death this way we know that it is natural to die.

But since God made people to live, to die is unnatural. Death is the penalty for sin. It is the last enemy for people to overcome.

Jesus raised people from the dead. He showed that He is the Lord of life. He overcame death for us when He died on the cross and arose again from the dead. When God calls people to have faith in Jesus He gives them spiritual life. They live close to God forever. This is the full life which Jesus gives to those who trust in Him.

TO HELP US REMEMBER

Jesus said:

✠ "The thief comes only to steal and kill and destroy; I came that they may have life and have it abundantly."

John 10:10

At our baptism Jesus came to live in us.

What does Baptism mean for daily living?

It means that our sinful self, with all its evil deeds and desires, should be drowned through daily repentance; and that day after day a new self should arise to live with God in righteousness and purity forever.

St. Paul writes in Romans 6: "We were buried therefore with Him by Baptism into death, so that as Christ was raised from the dead by the glory of the Father, we too might walk in newness of life."

WHAT THIS MEANS TO ME

When I sin I earn the wages of death. This is the punishment I deserve because I have disobeyed God. But God's free gift to me is eternal life. God grants this life through my faith in Jesus. He assures me that He has forgiven my sin through His death on the cross. He promised that I will rise from the dead because of His resurrection. He is my resurrection and life.

I will trust Jesus in life and death. He will be my strength against temptations to sin. He will help me overcome the fear of dying. He promises to take me into His presence to be with God forever.

MY PRAYER

Gracious God, I pray that You will not hold my sins against me nor refuse to hear me because of them. I daily sin much and deserve nothing but punishment. For Jesus' sake, instead of the death I have earned, give me the life which He earned for me.   AMEN.

Jesus, I live to Thee,
The Loveliest and Best;
My life in Thee, Thy life in me,
In Thy blest love I rest.

Living or dying, Lord,
I ask but to be Thine;
My life in Thee, Thy life in me,
Make Heaven forever mine.

The Lutheran Hymnal 591, st. 1, 4

35

WHEN JESUS WAS TRANSFIGURED

the glory of the Lord was upon Him

GOD AT WORK

The disciples of Jesus could not look Him in the face. He was brighter than the sun.

Jesus had led Peter, James, and John up a high mountain. The four of them were all by themselves. Then a blazing light suddenly flashed at the disciples. They covered their eyes. They could not look at it. The light came from Jesus.

The face of Jesus shone like the sun. His clothes sparkled with white light.

In a moment Moses and Elijah appeared. They talked with Jesus. They spoke of His plan to go to Jerusalem. There He would die on the cross to restore sinners to life with God. God had rescued His people out of Egypt many years before. Now God would rescue all people from sin through the life, death, and resurrection of Jesus, His Son.

The eyes of the disciples were so heavy they could hardly keep them open. They were tired. But they struggled against sleep. They saw the bright glory of Jesus. They saw the two men who stood with Him.

The men started to leave Jesus. Peter said, "Lord, it's so good to be here! Let's make three tents here. One will be for you, one for Moses, and one for Elijah." Peter wanted this happy moment to last for a long time.

As Peter talked a bright cloud hovered over them. A voice spoke from the cloud. "This is my beloved Son," the heavenly Father said. "I am well pleased with Him. Listen to Him."

God had startled the disciples with His voice from the cloud. They fell on their faces. They were afraid.

Luke 9

155

Jesus came and touched them with His hand. "Stand up," He invited. "Do not be afraid." When the disciples looked up they saw no one else. Jesus was alone.

A CLOSER LOOK

At His transfiguration Jesus revealed Himself as the Son of God. Also in His miracles He had made Himself known as God's Son. But this time God called Jesus His Son.

The glory of the Lord was upon Jesus. God wanted the disciples to know that their King was with them. God's kingdom is in the midst of His people when the King is among them. The greatest glory of the King is that He loved us so much that He was willing to die for us.

Jesus did not accept Peter's offer to build tents. They were not to stay on the mountain.

TO HELP US REMEMBER

Peter later wrote about his experience at the transfiguration of Jesus. He said:

> ✠ For we did not follow cleverly devised myths when we made known to you the power and coming of our Lord Jesus Christ, but we were eyewitnesses of His majesty. For when He received honor and glory from God the Father and the voice was borne to Him by the Majestic Glory, "This is my beloved Son, with whom I am well pleased," we heard this voice borne from heaven, for we were with Him on the holy mountain. *2 Peter 1:16-18*

In the *Second Article* of the Apostles' Creed we confess our faith that Jesus is God's Son. "I believe in Jesus Christ, His only Son, our Lord." In Luther's explanation to the Second Article we gladly confess that we belong to Jesus, our Lord. "I believe that Jesus Christ—true God, Son of the Father from eternity, and true man, born of the Virgin Mary—is my Lord."

156

WHAT THIS MEANS TO ME

Jesus' transfiguration shows that God lives among people in His Son. At His transfiguration Jesus looked forward to His death, resurrection, and coming again at the end of the world. Now this one event remains for the future: Jesus will return to give me the glory He earned for me.

God strengthened the faith of the disciples in Jesus. So God builds up my faith as He shows me the glory of Jesus. Jesus is the perfect Savior. He obeyed His Father in heaven all the way to His death on the cross for my sins.

"Listen to Jesus," my heavenly Father has taught me. Jesus has the words of eternal life. My present and my future are with Him. I must hear Him speak to me in His Word.

MY PRAYER

Thank You, heavenly Father, for showing Your glory in Christ Jesus. As You helped the disciples, I pray that You will help me to hold fast to my Savior. When I am unhappy or discouraged make me strong again. When I am tempted to doubt or to betray You through disobedience, help me overcome my sin. Open my heart so that I may listen to Jesus and follow Him as His witness.

AMEN.

'Tis good, Lord, to be here,
Thy glory fills the night;
Thy face and garments, like the sun,
Shine with unborrowed light.

Fulfiller of the past,
Promise of Things to be,
We hail Thy body glorified
And our redemption see.

'Tis good, Lord, to be here.
Yet we may not remain;
But since Thou biddest us leave the mount,
Come with us to the plain.

The Lutheran Hymnal 135, st. 1, 3, 5

PETER

ANDREW

JAMES the LESS

JOHN

PHILIP

THOMAS

36

WHEN JESUS BLESSED HIS APOSTLES

He built the church on Himself

GOD AT WORK

Jesus Christ founded the Christian church. This is the story of how Jesus told His plans for the church to the apostles.

They were all in the city called Caesarea. Suddenly Jesus asked the question, "Who do men say that the Son of Man is?"

The apostles gave different answers. "Some say that You are John the Baptizer. Others think You are the prophet Elijah, and still others think You are Jeremiah, or another prophet."

"But who do *you* say I am?" asked Jesus of the apostles.

Simon Peter replied for the Twelve: "You are the Christ, the Son of the living God."

"How blessed you are, Simon, son of Jona! My heavenly Father has revealed this truth to you. I tell you, you are Peter, a rock. I will build My church on this rock. My church will be so strong that even the powers of hell will not be able to harm it."

"I will give you the keys of the kingdom of heaven," Jesus said to the apostles. "Whatever you bind on earth shall be bound in heaven, and whatever you loose on earth shall be loosed in heaven."

In these words Jesus blessed His apostles. These were His gracious plans for His church.

Matthew 16

A CLOSER LOOK

"I believe in the holy Christian church, the communion of saints." Christians confess these words of the Apostles' Creed. The church is Christian because our Lord founded the church. He is the Christ, the Messiah, the Anointed One of God who completed the work of salvation. Whoever believes and confesses, "Jesus Christ is my Lord," is a member of the communion of saints, the Christian church.

Jesus chose His 12 men to teach and proclaim the Gospel of salvation. The Twelve were Simon Peter, Andrew, James and John the sons of Zebedee, Philip, Thomas, Bartholomew, Matthew, James the son of Alphaeus, Simon the Zealot, Judas the son of James, and Judas Iscariot.

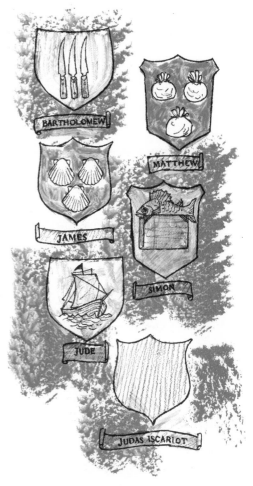

Not only were these apostles to announce the forgiveness of sin which unlocks the door of heaven, they were also to warn of eternal death to impenitent sinners. When a sinner wants to stay in his sin and refuses to believe the Gospel, the door to heaven is locked to him.

The Christian church is made up of all people who believe and confess: "Jesus Christ is my Lord." Jesus gives the believers in the church the power to proclaim and apply the Gospel of forgiveness which unlocks the door to heaven and to warn against impenitence which locks heaven's door.

159

TO HELP US REMEMBER

Jesus repeated this blessing and commission to His disciples on another occasion:

✠ "Receive the Holy Spirit. If you forgive the sins of any, they are forgiven; if you retain the sins of any, they are retained."
John 20:22b-23

St. James urges Christians:

✠ "Confess your sins to one another, and pray for one another."
James 5:16

What is private confession?

Private confession has two parts. First, we make a personal confession of sins to the pastor, and then we receive absolution, which means forgiveness as from God Himself. This absolution we should not doubt, but firmly believe that thereby our sins are forgiven before God in heaven.

What sins should we confess?

Before God we should confess that we are guilty of all sins, even those which are not known to us, as we do in the Lord's Prayer. But in private confession, as before the pastor, we should confess only those sins which trouble us in heart and mind.

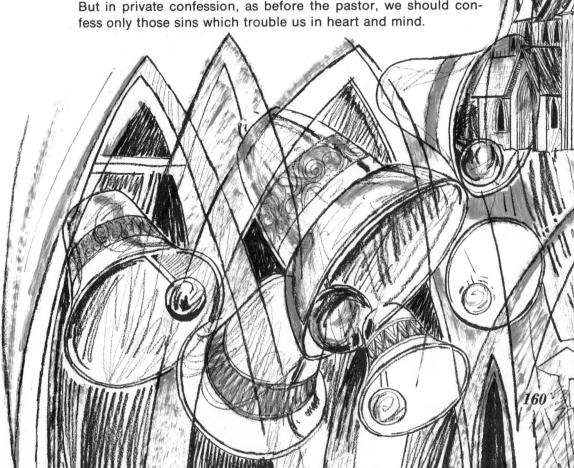

WHAT THIS MEANS TO ME

I believe that Jesus Christ is my Lord. I make this confession because God's Holy Spirit has called me by the Gospel. He has given me the true faith. I can be sure that I am His child because He made me a member of the church by Baptism.

I believe in the holy Christian church, the communion of saints. I belong to God's family together with all people who have been called by the Gospel. Jesus promises me that His church will last forever.

I believe that I do the church's work when I witness to the Gospel of Jesus Christ. I give my most effective witness when I tell penitent sinners that God forgives them for Jesus' sake and when I act in a forgiving spirit to my fellowmen.

MY PRAYER

O Lord of the church, I pray, send Your Holy Spirit so that many people may hear the Gospel and be converted from their sin. Make me a faithful witness to my Lord. Give me courage to confess my faith everywhere—even before scoffers and unbelievers. Give me Your love that I may treat others in a true spirit of forgiveness.

AMEN.

Built on the Rock the church doth stand
Even when steeples are falling;
Crumbled have spires in every land,
Bells still are chiming and calling,
Calling the young and old to rest,
But above all the soul distrest,
Longing for rest everlasting.

Grant, then, O God, where'er men roam,
That, when the church bells are ringing,
Many in saving faith may come
Where Christ His message is bringing:
"I know Mine own, Mine own know Me;
Ye, not the world, My face shall see.
My peace I leave with you." Amen.

The Lutheran Hymnal 467, st. 1, 7

37

WHEN JESUS ENTERED JERUSALEM

He was received as the Messiah King

GOD AT WORK

One Sunday the people of Jerusalem saw a thrilling parade.
The day before Jesus had visited in the home of Mary,
Martha, and Lazarus. They lived in the village of Bethany
which was not far from Jerusalem. That next day Jesus walked
to Jerusalem. Many people walked along with Him. These
people remembered His miracle of raising Lazarus from the
dead.

Matthew 21
Zechariah 9:9

Before He came to Jerusalem, He stopped. Calling two of the disciples to Him, He said, "Go to that village. As soon as you enter it, you will see a donkey and a colt. Untie them and bring them here to Me. If anyone asks you what you are doing, just tell him, 'Our Master needs these.' He will let you take them."

The disciples did just as Jesus asked them. They found the animals and brought them to Jesus. Jesus sat on the donkey. He wanted to ride into Jerusalem on this humble beast.

The parade into Jerusalem began. The crowds of people who had been following Jesus were joined by many more people from the city. As they saw Jesus, they cheered and sang. Many people took their clothes and laid them on the road where Jesus would ride. Others cut down palm branches and laid them on the road.

The shouts of the crowd rang through the air as they followed Jesus into the city: "Hosanna to the Son of David! Blessed be He who comes in the name of the Lord! Hosanna in the highest!" They kept shouting these words over and over.

This parade stirred the people of the city. "Who is this who is causing all the excitement?" they asked.

People in the crowds answered the question. "This is the prophet Jesus from Nazareth of Galilee."

A CLOSER LOOK

This is the story of the first Palm Sunday. The Lord made His last trip to Jerusalem before He died on the cross. But His entrance into the city was so different from the things which happened to Him during that week. The crowds of people confessed that He was the Son of David. They meant that Jesus was a king of the line of great King David. When they shouted, "Hosanna!" they were saying, "Save us, Lord!"

The prophet Zechariah had foretold this thrilling parade many years earlier. Matthew includes the words of his prophecy: "Tell the daughter of Zion, behold your King is coming to you, humble, and riding on a donkey." Jesus fulfilled these words.

TO HELP US REMEMBER

When we confess our faith in Jesus we say, "Jesus is my King." Martin Luther's explanation of the *Second Article* of the Apostles' Creed describes Jesus' work to bring sinners into His kingdom of grace.

> I believe that Jesus Christ—true God, Son of the Father from eternity, and true man, born of the Virgin Mary—is my Lord. At great cost He has saved and redeemed me, a lost and condemned person. He has freed me from sin, death, and the power of the devil—not with silver or gold, but with His holy and precious blood and His innocent suffering and death. All this He has done that I may be His own, live under Him in His kingdom, and serve Him in everlasting righteousness, innocence, and blessedness, just as He is risen from the dead and lives and rules eternally. This is most certainly true.

What is this kingdom over which Jesus rules? We find an answer to this question in Luther's explanation to the *Second Petition* of the Our Father

> **Thy kingdom come.**
>
> What does this mean?
>
> God's kingdom comes indeed without our praying for it, but we ask in this prayer that it may come also to us.
>
> When does this happen?
>
> God's kingdom comes when our heavenly Father gives us His Holy Spirit, so that by His grace we believe His holy Word and live a godly life on earth now and in heaven forever.

The key word here is "believe." Only by faith do we "know" God's kingdom or become a part of it. Jesus rules His kingdom by His love and grace. All His subjects are His own dear children.

WHAT THIS MEANS TO ME

When I think of the parades I may see, it's hard for me to imagine the Palm Sunday parade as a thrilling event. Today people can do so many more surprising things to make a parade thrilling and exciting. Jesus must not have looked like a mighty ruler as He rode on the back of a donkey.

But in faith I see Jesus' humble entrance into Jerusalem as the picture of my true King. It was Jesus, the Son of God, who listened to the shout of praise, "Hosanna to the Son of David, blessed is He that comes in the name of the Lord!" It was Jesus who a few days later died on the cross, and three days later He rose from the dead.

Jesus is my King. He conquered all my enemies for me. He will keep me in His kingdom here on earth and take me to His heavenly kingdom when I die.

MY PRAYER

Give me faith to believe that You are my King,
O Lord Jesus. Help me fight the temptations to
worship false kings in my life. Help me do what
I can to bring others into Thy kingdom.

AMEN.

All glory, laud, and honor
To Thee, Redeemer, King,
To whom the lips of children
Made sweet hosannas ring.
Thou art the King of Israel,
Thou David's royal Son
Who in the Lord's name comest,
The King and Blessed One.

All glory, laud, and honor
To Thee, Redeemer, King,
To whom the lips of children
Made sweet hosannas ring.
Thou didst accept their praises;
Accept the prayers we bring,
Who in all good delightest,
Thou good and gracious King.

The Lutheran Hymnal 160, st. 1, 5

38

WHEN JESUS WASHED
THE DISCIPLES' FEET

He taught them how to love one another

GOD AT WORK

Jesus is King of all. But Jesus is also a servant. On Sunday Jesus made a grand entrance into Jerusalem. Then on Thursday Jesus acted like a servant.

He and the 12 apostles were at supper together. It was in a quiet room in the home of a friend of Jesus. As they were eating the Passover supper together, right in the middle of the meal, Jesus rose from the table. He took off His robe and laid it aside. He tied a towel around His waist. He looked just like a servant now. Then He poured water into a bowl. As the startled disciples watched, He began to wash their feet. Then He wiped them with a towel.

He came to Simon Peter to wash his feet. Peter stopped Jesus with the question, "Lord, do You wash my feet?"

"You do not understand what I am doing now," Jesus answered. "But you will understand someday."

"I'm not going to let You wash my feet," insisted Peter.

Jesus said, "If I do not wash you, you do not belong to Me."

"Lord, then wash my hands and my head too!" exclaimed Peter.

But Jesus told him that would not be necessary. He finished washing the feet of all the apostles.

Then He put on His robe again and sat down at the table.

"Do you understand what I have done for you? You call me 'Teacher' and 'Lord.' You are right. That's who I am. If I, your Teacher and Lord, have washed your feet, you also ought to

wash one another's feet. This is My example for you. You must
remember that the servant is not above his master.''

Jesus showed His love for His disciples even to the last days
of His life on earth.

A CLOSER LOOK

Jesus must have surprised His apostles when He began to wash their feet. He was their Master. But He did something only a servant should do. In this way Jesus showed that He came to be a servant. He was a king, too, but in humility. He came to serve, not to be served.

He did the servant's job for His disciples because He loved them so dearly. Before the next day would end, the disciples would see Jesus' greatest act of love. He would die on the cross.

All who follow the Master and receive His great love are happy to show love and concern for their fellowmen. This is not easy to do—especially to one who has hurt us. But Jesus shows us that to love means to be a servant.

TO HELP US REMEMBER

Jesus teaches us love for our fellowman in the Our Father. We pray for each other in this prayer. In the *Fifth Petition* we also forgive our fellowman any wrong he may have committed against us.

And forgive us our trespasses, as we forgive those who trespass against us.

What does this mean?

We ask in this prayer that our Father in heaven would not hold our sins against us and because of them refuse to hear our prayer. And we pray that He would give us everything by grace, for we sin every day and deserve nothing but punishment. So we on our part will heartily forgive and gladly do good to those who sin against us.

In this petition we pray God to be as forgiving to us as we are to others. God forgives us an unpayable debt because Jesus offered His life for us on the cross. In His love we find it possible to say to someone, "I forgive you too."

When James and John selfishly asked for seats of honor in glory, Jesus taught them a special lesson on being a servant.

✠"Whoever would be great among you must be your servant, and whoever would be first among you must be slave of all. For the Son of Man also came not to be served, but to serve and to give His life as a ransom for many."

Mark 10:43b-45

WHAT THIS MEANS TO ME

God has called me into His kingdom to serve. The King is Jesus Christ, Teacher and Lord. But Jesus was also the Servant. His example of washing the disciples' feet reminds me of the way I can show concern for other people. I should show this especially to those whom I am tempted to dislike or even hate.

But it is not only Jesus' example which moves me to do this. It is because I belong to Him by Baptism. This is the way a disciple of the Master wants to live. I pray that God would always help me remember who I am.

MY PRAYER

Thank You, gracious Savior, for calling me into Your kingdom. Your forgiveness for my sins cleanses me. You have prepared me to serve You as a disciple. Teach me to conquer my selfish desires. Make me able to love others and serve them in humble obedience to You.

AMEN.

O God of mercy, God of might,
In love and pity infinite,
Teach us, as ever in Thy sight,
To live our life to Thee.

Teach us the lesson Thou hast taught,
To feel for those Thy blood hath bought,
That every word and deed and thought
May work a work for Thee.

And may Thy Holy Spirit move
All those who live to live in love
Till Thou shalt greet in heaven above
All those who live to Thee.

The Lutheran Hymnal 439, st. 1, 3, 6

39

WHEN JESUS ATE THE PASSOVER

He instituted His Holy Supper

GOD AT WORK

Jesus gave His people a precious gift before He died. This gift is His Holy Supper.

It all happened the night Jesus ate the Passover meal with His disciples. For many hundreds of years God's people remembered the time when the blood of the Passover lamb saved lives. God saved Israel from the angel of death and freed them from slavery in Egypt. Each year the Israelites ate the Passover meal to celebrate that great event.

"Lord, where shall we eat the Passover?" asked the disciples.

"Go to a certain man in the city," Jesus replied. "Tell him that the Master wishes to keep the Passover in his house." The disciples did as Jesus asked. They prepared the meal.

That night they ate the Passover meal. While they were eating, Jesus took some of the bread, prayed a prayer of thanks, and broke the bread in pieces.

"Take, eat," He said as He gave it to the disciples. "This is My body. It is given for you."

Then He took a cup of wine. Again He prayed a thanksgiving prayer and gave it to the disciples.

"Drink of it, all of you. This is My blood of the new covenant. It is poured out for the forgiveness of your sins. Each time that you celebrate this Holy Supper, you shall remember Me and My work of redemption."

A CLOSER LOOK

To this very day Christians remember the death of the Lord Jesus Christ by eating this sacred meal. When we come to the altar to partake of Holy Communion, Jesus Himself is present to serve us. In this wonderful way Jesus binds Himself to His people.

Jesus replaced the Passover meal of the old covenant with His Holy Supper. God's people of the Old Testament found strength in remembering the act of God through the blood of the Passover lamb. God's people of the New Testament remember the sacrifice of the Lamb of God, Jesus Christ.

We cannot explain how we receive Jesus' body and blood in this Holy Supper. We simply believe Jesus when He promises us forgiveness for all our sins. He makes this faith strong when we receive His body and blood in the Sacrament.

171

TO HELP US REMEMBER

We may ask ourselves four questions to help us remember why Jesus wants us to celebrate His Holy Supper.

What is Holy Communion?

Holy Communion is the body and blood of our Lord Jesus Christ given with bread and wine, instituted by Christ Himself for us to eat and drink.

Where do the Scriptures say this?

Matthew, Mark, Luke, and Paul say:

Our Lord Jesus Christ, in the night in which He was betrayed, took bread; and when He had given thanks, He broke it and gave it to His disciples, saying, "Take, eat; this is My body, which is given for you; this do in remembrance of Me."

After the same manner also He took the cup after supper, and when He had given thanks, He gave it to them, saying, "Drink of it, all of you; this cup is the new testament in My blood, which is shed for you and for many for the remission of sins; this do, as often as you drink it, in remembrance of Me."

What benefits do we receive from this sacrament?

The benefits of this sacrament are pointed out by the words, *given and shed for you for the remission of sins.* These words assure us that in the sacrament we receive forgiveness of sins, life, and salvation. For where there is forgiveness of sins, there is also life and salvation.

How can eating and drinking do all this?

It is not eating and drinking that does this, but the words, *given and shed for you for the remission of sins.* These words, along with eating and drinking, are the main thing in the sacrament. And whoever believes these words has exactly what they say, forgiveness of sins.

172

WHAT THIS MEANS TO ME

Every time my congregation celebrates Holy Communion, God makes it a happy event. He brings Jesus' saving death on the cross into the life of each believer. Jesus says, "This is *for you*. I shed My blood *for you*. I forgive you all your sins."

Jesus gives His body and blood in and with the bread and wine. He Himself is present to reveal the love God has for us. I am thankful to God for bringing His people together to share His love in the new covenant meal. I am looking forward to the time when I can receive the special gifts God offers in His Holy Supper.

MY PRAYER

> Thank You, Lord Jesus, for Your Holy Supper.
> Help me and my congregation honor You in each
> Communion celebration. Make my faith strong to
> turn away from every sin as I keep turning to You
> for forgiveness.
>
> AMEN.

An awe-full mystery is here
To challenge faith and waken fear:
The Savior comes as food divine,
Concealed in earthly bread and wine.

Lord, show us still that Thou art good
And grant us evermore this food.
Give faith to every wavering soul
And make each wounded spirit whole.

The Lutheran Hymnal 304, st. 1, 6

173

40

WHEN JESUS PRAYED

He revealed Himself as our High Priest

GOD AT WORK

Jesus prayed often. He taught His disciples to pray. The night when He ate the Passover with His disciples, He prayed a special prayer. He knew He would die soon. He knew that His work was coming to an end. In this prayer He did not pray for Himself, but for His disciples and for us. In this prayer especially He reveals Himself as the great High Priest of sinners.

There had been many high priests before Jesus came into the world. Long before Jesus' time God had told His people about the work of the priests. They were to talk to Him for the people. God described the various sacrifices they were to offer. He instructed them how a man was to be ordained as a priest. He also told them what the priest should wear when he was performing his sacrifices.

One of the greatest days for the high priest was the Day of Atonement. This was the only time in the year that God permitted the high priest to go behind the curtain into the holiest place in the temple. If any man entered there at any other time he would die. The priest washed himself and put on special clothing. Then he made the sacrifice for the Day of Atonement according to God's command. He took the blood of a goat with him to sprinkle on the mercy seat which was in the holiest place behind the veil.

What an exciting day this was for the people of Israel. It was the day they awaited anxiously. They felt the burden of their many sins. They wanted to know that God had forgiven them all

John 17
Hebrews 9

their sins. The high priest was an important person to speak to God for them and then tell them what God had said. They knew that if God was displeased, the high priest might even die. When the day arrived, all the people gathered outside the temple porch. They watched him walk solemnly in all his beautiful robes into the temple. Then they knew he was walking behind the curtains which covered the holiest place. God was in that room! Would He listen to the high priest's prayers for forgiveness? Would God accept the offering of the blood? Would He forgive?

The people waited anxiously. Suddenly the high priest appeared on the porch again! They shouted with joy, for this was the sign that God had forgiven them their sins.

When Jesus prayed to His Father, He showed that He is our High Priest. He did not pray for Himself. He made Himself the sacrifice and shed His own blood so that He could talk to God for all sinners. He was the greatest High Priest. He did not have to go into this holiest place each year. When He gave His life on the cross, He fulfilled perfectly all the sacrifices which Old Testament high priests offered each year in the holiest place of the temple.

175

A CLOSER LOOK

Jesus is our High Priest today, too. Even to this day He talks to God for sinners. He rose from the dead to show that He was the greatest High Priest. Sinners can pray to God Almighty through their High Priest, Jesus Christ. They can be sure that God will hear their prayers and forgive them their sins.

TO HELP US REMEMBER

We should try to remember some of the precious words which Jesus spoke in His great high-priestly prayer which He prayed the night in which He was betrayed.

> ✠ "I do not pray for these only, but also for those who are to believe in Me through their word, that they may all be one; even as Thou, Father, art in Me, and I in Thee, that they also may be in Us, so that the world may believe that Thou hast sent Me." *John 17:20-21*

> "I made known to them Thy name, and I will make it known, that the love with which Thou hast loved Me may be in them, and I in them." *John 17:26*

Because of our High Priest we can pray to God in His name. In the opening words of His prayer Jesus taught us how to pray to God with confidence:

Our Father who art in heaven.

What does this mean?

Here God encourages us to believe that He is truly our Father and we are His children. We therefore are to pray to Him with complete confidence just as children speak to their loving father.

176

WHAT THIS MEANS TO ME

When I think of my many sins I am afraid. I am afraid of God's punishment. When I am afraid, I don't feel like praying to God.

But Jesus is my High Priest. This means that He will ask God to forgive me all my sins. I know that God will do this. When Jesus died on the cross He made the one sacrifice which is enough for all men's sins. This makes God my Father!

Now I can pray the Our Father with more understanding and confidence. For Jesus' sake my prayers have all been answered.

MY PRAYER

I praise You, O Father, for sending Jesus to be my High Priest. I praise You, O Lord Jesus, for Your suffering and death. I praise You, O Holy Spirit, for making me God's child and giving me faith to believe. Thank You, almighty God, for the privilege of praying in the name of my High Priest, Jesus Christ.

AMEN.

Father of heaven, whose love profound
A ransom for our souls hath found,
Before Thy throne we sinners bend;
To us Thy pardoning love extend.

Almighty Son, Incarnate Word,
Our Prophet, Priest, Redeemer, Lord,
Before Thy throne we sinners bend;
To us Thy saving grace extend.

Eternal Spirit, by whose breath
The soul is raised from sin and death,
Before Thy throne we sinners bend;
To us Thy quickening power extend.

The Lutheran Hymnal 242, st. 1, 2, 3

177

41

WHEN JESUS SUFFERED
IN THE GARDEN . . .

He showed that He is a true human being

GOD AT WORK

Jesus was sad.

After singing a hymn with His disciples Jesus went with them out of the city to a garden called Gethsemane. He knew that soon men would take Him prisoner. They would mock Him and torture Him. They would kill Him.

Jesus wanted to pray to His Father. He told His disciples, "Sit here. I am going over there to pray." Then Jesus took Peter, James, and John with Him a little farther into the garden.

"I am very sad," Jesus said. "My heart is ready to break. Stay here. Watch with Me."

Jesus went on a little and fell on His knees to pray. "My Father," He said, "if it is possible, take My suffering away. But do Your will."

Jesus stood up and went back to the three disciples. All three were fast asleep.

Jesus woke them up. "What are you doing?" He said to Peter. "Could none of you stay awake with Me for one hour? Stay awake. Pray, so that you will not be tempted."

Jesus went away a second time. He prayed, "My Father, if it is not possible for this cup of suffering to pass Me by without My drinking it, Your will be done."

Once more Jesus returned to His disciples. He found them asleep again.

Jesus left the disciples a third time. He prayed again using the same words as before. He thought of the punishment He must bear for the sins of people everywhere. He began to suffer the pains of the death He must die. The drops of sweat on His forehead became drops of blood. Then an angel came down from the Father in heaven to comfort Him and make Him strong.

"Still sleeping?" He asked the disciples when He came back to them again. "Still taking your rest? The time has come. The Son of Man is betrayed into the hands of sinful men. Get up, let us go. The traitor is close by."

A CLOSER LOOK

Jesus suffered. He was a true human being. He took the punishment for our sins into His own body. He was under the curse which we deserved because we have disobeyed God.

In the Garden of Gethsemane Jesus felt pain. Satan tried to make Him think that His Father had forgotten Him. Otherwise, why would God allow Him to suffer so?

179

But Jesus conquered Satan. He obeyed His Father's will and continued His way to the cross to die for us. As a true human being, He is our perfect "substitute." Because of His death God has set us free from sin. The man Christ Jesus gave Himself willingly as a ransom for us all.

TO HELP US REMEMBER

Jesus was not play-acting in Gethsemane. He suffered real pain. He knew how He would have to die. He said to His disciples:

> "My soul is very sorrowful, even to death; remain here, and watch with Me."
> *Matthew 26:38*

> [Jesus] prayed, "My Father, if it be possible, let this cup pass from Me; nevertheless, not as I will, but as Thou wilt."
> *Matthew 26:39*

Jesus did not let the suffering turn Him away from His assignment. He did not fail His Father. But the disciples failed Jesus. Jesus warned them:

> "So, could you not watch with Me one hour? Watch and pray that you may not enter into temptation; the spirit indeed is willing, but the flesh is weak."
> *Matthew 26:40b-41*

In the Our Father we pray that God will make us strong to do His will as we pray in the *Third Petition*.

Thy will be done on earth as it is in heaven.

What does this mean?

The good and gracious will of God is surely done without our prayer, but we ask in this prayer that it may be done also among us.

When does this happen?

God's will is done when He hinders and defeats every evil scheme and purpose of the devil, the world, and our sinful self, which would prevent us from keeping His name holy and would oppose the coming of His kingdom. And His will is done when He strengthens our faith and keeps us firm in His Word as long as we live. This is His gracious and good will.

WHAT THIS MEANS TO ME

Jesus was a human being as I am, except He was without sin. When He was born, He became man so that He could really suffer the bitter pains in the Garden of Gethsemane for me. This is included in what the Christmas angel meant when he announced, "Unto you is born this day in the city of David a Savior." I praise and love my Savior for suffering for me.

He teaches me to pray the same prayer He prayed in His suffering. I pray, "Thy will be done." Jesus helps me to accept God's plans and promises for my daily life. And when I am in trouble, I pray that God's will may be done for me.

MY PRAYER

> Gracious Father, conquer every evil scheme which would not let Your will be done in me. Make my faith in Jesus strong and keep me firm in Your Word and promises. Teach me to know Your will and to follow my Lord Jesus Christ in carrying it out in all things. For His name's sake.
>
> AMEN.

My God, my Father, make me strong,
When tasks of life seem hard and long,
To greet them with this triumph song:
Thy will be done.

Draw from my timid eyes the veil
To show, where earthly forces fail,
Thy power and love must still prevail—
Thy will be done.

The Lutheran Hymnal 424, st. 1, 2

181

42

WHEN JESUS WAS BETRAYED

He showed Himself as the promised
Suffering Servant

GOD AT WORK

God had said that He would build His kingdom through His Servant. His Servant would suffer many seeming defeats. He would die, but through Him and His obedience God would forgive the sins of all people.

Jesus is that Suffering Servant of God.

While He was still in the Garden of Gethsemane talking with His disciples, Judas walked up to Him. A large crowd followed Judas. They carried swords and clubs. Jesus' enemies had sent them.

Judas had given the mob with him a signal. "The man you want is the one I will kiss. Grab Him." Stepping up to Jesus, Judas said, "Hail, Master!" and kissed Him.

Jesus replied, "Friend, what are you here for? Are you betraying the Son of Man with a kiss?" Then some men from the crowd grabbed Jesus.

Peter thought he must defend His Master. Reaching for his sword he swung it and cut off a man's ear. But Jesus said to Peter, "Put your sword away where it belongs. My Father would send a thousand angels to help Me if I asked Him. But that is not what I want. I must be taken captive by these men. The Scriptures must be fulfilled." Then Jesus healed the man's ear.

Jesus spoke to the crowd. "Do you think I am a robber? I see you have brought your swords and clubs. When I taught in the temple you did not try to hurt me. But all this has happened so that the prophets' words will come true."

The disciples left Jesus and ran away. He faced His enemies alone.

Isaiah 53
Matthew 26

They took Him to the house of Caiaphas, the high priest. They tried to find some reason to put Him to death. One man claimed that Jesus had made this boast: "If you destroy the temple of God, I can build it up again in three days." The high priest asked Jesus whether He had said that. Jesus didn't say a word.

"Are you the Messiah?" the high priest demanded.

"I am," Jesus said. "One day you will see the Son of Man seated on the right hand of God and coming with the clouds of heaven."

"This is enough!" the high priest said. "He has blasphemed God. What should we do with Him?"

"He is guilty of death," they answered.

183

A CLOSER LOOK

Did Jesus suffer because He had sinned? No! He was innocent. He suffered because we sinned. This was God's plan: that Jesus suffer for sinners. The prophets had said that He would redeem sinners for eternal life with God. When Jesus suffered willingly for others, He fulfilled what the prophets had promised.

TO HELP US REMEMBER

Jesus knew why He had to suffer. That's why He said to the crowd:

> ✵"But all this has taken place, that the Scriptures of the prophets might be fulfilled." *Matthew 26:56a*

One of the prophets who foretold Jesus' great suffering and agony was Isaiah. (See Lesson 27.) He described God's Suffering Servant, and Jesus was the One who fit His description.

> ✵We esteemed Him stricken, smitten by God, and afflicted . . . and the Lord has laid on Him the iniquity of us all . . . it was the will of the Lord to bruise Him.
> *Isaiah 53:4b, 6b, 10a*

In the Our Father we ask God to make us strong to fight temptation. (Judas listened to Satan's temptation and sinned.) In the *Sixth Petition* we ask for help.

And lead us not into temptation.

What does this mean?

God tempts no one to sin, but we ask in this prayer that God would watch over us and keep us so that the devil, the world, and our sinful self may not deceive us and draw us into false belief, despair, and other great and shameful sins. And we pray that even though we are so tempted we may still win the final victory.

WHAT THIS MEANS TO ME

My salvation is sure! God's Suffering Servant, promised by Isaiah, died and rose again for me. He is Jesus, God's own Son. God kept His word.

I have often betrayed my Lord. I have refused to follow Him closely. I have not always obeyed God's will for me. Now I turn to God for His forgiveness and trust Jesus' work for me.

Now I know that to serve God may mean to suffer for Him. God has made me His child so that I may tell His glory to all people. Sometimes it may mean to give up what I would like to do. But I will keep telling others of His love and forgiveness in Jesus so that together we may trust Him in everything.

MY PRAYER

I thank You, gracious Father, for Your Suffering Servant who is my Savior. Grant me the faith to receive all His work as done for me. Make me willing to suffer for the sake of Your glory. Make me strong enough to win against every temptation which tries to separate me from You. Through Jesus I ask it.

AMEN.

Christ, the Life of all the living,
Christ, the Death of death, our foe,
Who, Thyself for me once giving
To the darkest depths of woe—
Through Thy sufferings, death, and merit
I eternal life inherit:
Thousand, thousand thanks shall be,
Dearest Jesus, unto Thee.

The Lutheran Hymnal 151, st. 1

185

43

WHEN JESUS WAS CONDEMNED

He suffered for our salvation

GOD AT WORK

"He is guilty of death!" These words were spoken by the Council, which had condemned the innocent Jesus to death. Now Jesus stood in another court. The Roman governor, Pontius Pilate, was the judge here.

Pilate questioned Jesus, "Are you the king of the Jews?"

"You have said so," Jesus replied.

The chief priests accused Jesus of many things. Since they were lies, Jesus did not answer. Pilate was surprised. "Aren't you going to reply to them?" But Jesus remained silent.

Pilate was sure that Jesus had done nothing wrong. He thought he knew of a way to release Him.

186

Pilate sent some of his men to the prison. They brought back a murderer by the name of Barabbas. Pilate put Barabbas next to Jesus. Then he said to the people:

"This is a special feast day for you. You know that on a day like this I release a prisoner you choose. Which of these two do you want me to release for you, Barabbas, or Jesus, who is called Christ?" He thought that surely they would choose Jesus. The chief priests and elders persuaded the people to ask for Barabbas.

Pilate asked them a second time, "Whom shall I let go?" "Barabbas!" they shouted. "Then what shall I do with Jesus?" They all said, "Let Him be crucified."

Pilate gave up. He didn't want to start a riot. But he still didn't think Jesus was guilty. So Pilate took a basin of water and washed his hands for everyone to see. He said, "I am innocent of this man's blood. See to it yourselves."

"His blood be on us and on our children," cried the people. Pilate released Barabbas.

The soldiers of the governor took Jesus into the palace. They stripped His clothes off Him. They threw an old scarlet robe over Him. They wove a crown out of thorn twigs and put it on His head. They put a stick in His hand. Kneeling in front of Him they mocked Him. "Hail to the King," they said. "What a fine king you have turned out to be."

Pilate placed the beaten and bleeding Jesus before the people and said, "Behold the Man!" But all Pilate's attempts to free Jesus were opposed by the people, who shouted "Crucify Him." Pilate gave in to the throng and handed Jesus over to be crucified.

Jesus had done nothing to fight back. He let them do what they wanted. Finally they put His own clothes back on Him. Then they led Him away to crucify Him.

A CLOSER LOOK

Why did God deliver His Son into the hands of evil men? Through His death God sealed the covenant He had made with His people. By the blood of His own Son, God granted the forgiveness which He had promised. Jesus gave up His life so that all people might have life with the Father. Jesus is the Lamb of God who takes away the world's sins.

TO HELP US REMEMBER

When Jesus permitted Himself to be condemned to death He did this as God's sacrifice for sinners. He was the sacrificial Lamb. God had pictured this Lamb to His people when He ordered them to eat the sacred meal of the Passover. The blood of the Passover lamb protected them from the angel of death. We read this in Exodus 12. (See Lesson 16.)

The prophet Isaiah described the Savior as a lamb condemned to die.

> He was oppressed, and He was afflicted, yet He opened not His mouth; like a lamb that is led to the slaughter, and like a sheep that before its shearers is dumb, so He opened not His mouth. *Isaiah 53:7*

John the Baptizer pointed to Jesus one day and announced:

> ✠ "Behold, the Lamb of God, who takes away the sin of the world!" *John 1:29*

Many years later Simon Peter also described Jesus as the Lamb of God.

> ✠ You know that you were ransomed from the futile ways inherited from your fathers, not with perishable things such as silver or gold, but with the precious blood of Christ, like that of a lamb without blemish or spot. *1 Peter 1:18-19*

St. John saw the glorious vision of heaven which he describes in the Book of Revelation. He saw the Son of God as the victorious Lamb, and he records the hymn of praise which the angels and elders sang:

"Worthy is the Lamb who was slain to receive power and wealth and wisdom and might and honor and glory and blessing!"
Revelation 5:12

WHAT THIS MEANS TO ME

"The wages of sin is death." Because of my sin I deserve eternal death.

"But the gift of God is eternal life through Jesus Christ my Lord." Instead of death, which I earned, God grants me the gift of His grace. He gives me life through Jesus Christ.

I believe that Jesus is the Lamb of God who died for my sins. I belong to this Savior. I live in His kingdom. My baptism is my assurance of His promise to keep me in His kingdom now and in eternity.

MY PRAYER

O Christ, Lamb of God, who takes away the sin of the world, have mercy upon me. Grant me Your peace.

AMEN.

This Lamb is Christ, the soul's great Friend,
The Lamb of God, our Savior;
Him God the Father chose to send
To gain for us His favor.
"Go forth, My Son," the Father saith,
"And free men from the fear of death,
From guilt and condemnation.
The wrath and stripes are hard to bear,
But by Thy Passion men shall share
The fruit of Thy salvation."

The Lutheran Hymnal 142, st. 2

44

WHEN JESUS WAS CRUCIFIED

He rescued us from all our enemies

GOD AT WORK

Pilate's soldiers led Jesus away to crucify Him. They made Him carry His own cross. But He was tired and weak because He had suffered so much. The cross was too heavy for Him. He stumbled and fell.

A soldier called to a man in the crowd. "Come and carry this cross!" The man's name was Simon. He was from Cyrene. He carried the cross for Jesus.

Leaving Jerusalem the crowd came to a hill called Golgotha. The name means "place of a skull." Here the soldiers nailed Jesus to the cross and stood it upright in the ground. Two other men were crucified there also. They were robbers.

In His first words from the cross Jesus prayed for His enemies. "Father, forgive them. They don't know what they are doing."

The people who passed by felt no pity for Jesus. "You claimed that You could pull the temple down and build it again in three days. If You are the Son of God, come down from the cross!"

The chief priests and elders jeered too. "He saved others, but He can't save Himself. If He comes down from the cross, we will believe Him. If God wants Him, let God rescue Him."

One of the robbers crucified with Jesus joined in the jeering. But the other said to him, "You and I deserve to be on this cross. But He has done nothing wrong." Then he said to Jesus, "Lord, think of me when You come into Your kingdom."

Matthew 27
Luke 23
John 19

The Savior replied, "Today you will be with Me in Paradise."

Jesus saw His mother and John at the foot of the cross. "Woman, see your new son." To John He said, "See your mother." From then on John took care of Mary as his mother.

Jesus was nailed to the cross at 9 o'clock in the morning. At noon darkness fell over the whole land. It stayed dark until 3 o'clock in the afternoon. About that time Jesus cried to His Father, "Eli, Eli, lama sabach-thani?" ("My God, My God, why have You forsaken Me?") Some of the people thought He was calling the prophet Elijah.

All the pain Jesus suffered dried up His throat. "I thirst," He said. A man put a sponge on a stick. He lifted it to Jesus' lips.

Then Jesus cried, "It is finished. Father, I give My spirit over to You."

With these words Jesus died. At that moment the heavy curtain in the temple ripped in two from top to bottom. An earthquake split rocks and opened graves. When the soldiers saw what happened, one of them said, "There is no doubt that this Man was the Son of God."

191

A CLOSER LOOK

The little hill called Calvary, just outside Jerusalem, is the most important place in the world. Here God finished His work of redemption. When Jesus was crucified, He suffered hell and death in our place. He rescued us from the power of Satan, sin, and death forever. This is why the cross is a central symbol for Christians.

TO HELP US REMEMBER

Our Lord spoke seven times from the cross. He said:

1. "Father, forgive them; for they know not what they do."
   Luke 23:34
2. To the penitent thief: "Truly, I say to you, today you will be with Me in Paradise."   *Luke 23:43*
3. He said to His mother: "Woman, behold your son!" Then He said to the disciple, "Behold your mother!"
   John 19:26-27
4. "Eli, Eli, lama sabach-thani?" that is, "My God, My God, why hast Thou forsaken Me?"   *Matthew 27:46*
5. To fulfill the Scriptures: "I thirst."   *John 19:28*
6. "It is finished."   *John 19:30*
7. "Father, into Thy hands I commit My spirit!"
   Luke 23:46

Luther's explanation to the *Second Article* expresses well our faith in Jesus.

At great cost He has saved and redeemed me, a lost and condemned person. He has freed me from sin, death, and the power of the devil—not with silver or gold, but with His holy and precious blood and His innocent suffering and death.

But if any one does sin, we have an Advocate with the Father, Jesus Christ the Righteous; and He is the Expiation for our sins, and not for ours only but also for the sins of the whole world.   *1 John 2:1b-2*

192

WHAT THIS MEANS TO ME

What a terrible enemy Satan is! He is cunning and sly and makes me sin before I know he is attacking me. He wants me to be unhappy. He wants me to make other people unhappy by being unkind to them. I am too weak to fight him alone and win.

Praise God, for He sent His Son to be a Conqueror for me in the war against Satan and all my enemies. When Jesus suffered and died on the cross, He completed His work of rescuing me from the power of Satan, sin, and death.

God protects me from Satan's temptations. He gives me the strength to live as His child. In Jesus' crucifixion, death, and resurrection I can conquer sin and death, and I look forward to eternal life in heaven.

MY PRAYER

Thank You, gracious Father, for my rescue from the devil and his power. I confess that I have not always trusted You to give me the victory over him. Forgive my weak faith. Increase in me the happy confidence that You protect me every day through Jesus' death.

AMEN.

Lord Jesus, we give thanks to Thee
That Thou hast died to set us free;
Made righteous through Thy precious blood,
We now are reconciled to God.

By virtue of Thy wounds we pray,
True God and Man, be Thou our Stay,
Our Comfort when we yield our breath,
Our Rescue from eternal death.

The Lutheran Hymnal 173, st. 1, 2

45

WHEN JESUS ROSE FROM THE DEAD

He conquered death

GOD AT WORK

Jesus' friends watched Him die on the cross. Then a man by the name of Joseph, from the city of Arimathea, called on Pilate in his palace. Pilate told him he could take Jesus' body from the cross and bury it. Joseph wrapped Jesus' body in a linen sheet. He laid it in his own tomb which was cut out of rock. No one else had ever been buried there.

Some women had followed Jesus from Galilee to Jerusalem. They saw how tenderly Joseph buried Him. Then they went home. They prepared spices and perfumes. On Saturday they rested. Very early Sunday morning they came to the tomb carrying their spices. They wanted to pour the perfumes over Jesus' body and place the sweet spices in the folds of the linen wrap. They thought this was His final resting place.

The women knew that a huge, round stone covered the opening to the tomb. They wondered who would roll it away for them. When they arrived at the grave they were astonished. The stone was rolled to one side. They could walk right in.

Mary from the city of Magdala didn't wait to see what was inside the tomb. She ran back to Jerusalem to find Peter and John. "They have taken the Lord's body out of the tomb," she reported. "We don't know where they have laid Him."

The other women went into the grave. Another surprise greeted them. The body of Jesus was nowhere in sight. All of a sudden two men in dazzling clothes were at their side. The women were terrified!

The angels said, "Why search among the dead for one who lives? You are looking for Jesus of Nazareth who was crucified. He is not here. He is risen. Remember what He told you while He was still in Galilee: 'The Son of Man must be handed over to sinful men, be crucified, and rise on the third day.' Now go quickly and tell His disciples that He is risen from the dead. Don't forget to tell Peter: 'Jesus is going ahead of you to Galilee. There you will see Him as He promised.'"

The women were Joanna and Mary the mother of James. They left the tomb and hurried away. They trembled with fear. They were stunned by their great joy. They ran to tell the news to the disciples. But the disciples thought their story was nonsense. They didn't believe the women's report.

195

A CLOSER LOOK

God conquered death for us. Jesus has destroyed its power. Death could not hold Him in the grave. He overcame our last great enemy.

The resurrection of Jesus was a sign from God. By that great miracle He announced that His plan to save people from sin was completed. The death and resurrection of Jesus brought men forgiveness. God gave His approval to all that Jesus had done in His suffering and sacrifice. Where God grants forgiveness for sin He grants eternal life and salvation.

TO HELP US REMEMBER

God explained the empty tomb in the message of the angel.

> ✠ "Do not be afraid; for I know that you seek Jesus who was crucified. He is not here; for He has risen, as He said. Come, see the place where He lay. Then go quickly and tell His disciples that He has risen from the dead, and behold, He is going before you to Galilee; there you will see Him." *Matthew 28:5-7*

In Adam's sin, death passed on to all of us because all of us have sinned. Jesus is God's Second Adam who destroyed the power of death for us in His resurrection.

> ✠ For as by a man came death, by a man has come also the resurrection of the dead. For as in Adam all die, so also in Christ shall all be made alive. *1 Corinthians 15:21-22*

In the *Second Article* of the Apostles' Creed we confess our faith in the risen and living Savior who brings about our redemption.

> **And in Jesus Christ, His only Son, our Lord; who was conceived by the Holy Ghost, born of the Virgin Mary; suffered under Pontius Pilate, was crucified, dead, and buried; He descended into hell; the third day He rose again from the dead; He ascended into heaven, and sitteth on the right hand of God the Father Almighty; from thence He shall come to judge the quick and the dead.**

WHAT THIS MEANS TO ME

My last great enemy is death. I deserve to be cut off eternally from God because I have sinned. Adam's sin of rebellion against God has become my own sin.

Jesus is God's Second Adam. He brought life to me when He overcame death for me. Now I no longer need to fear death. My risen and living Savior will take me by the hand. He will lead me into the presence of my Father in heaven.

Death could not hold my Jesus in the grave. He will not let death keep me in the grave. He will raise me up at the last day to life in heaven.

God brought Israel out of the slavery of Egypt. God has brought me out of the darkness of death into the light of life through the resurrection of His Son. So my faith and hope are fixed on God who raised Jesus from the dead.

MY PRAYER

Thank You, gracious Father, for declaring that Your Son Jesus is our Savior through His resurrection from the dead. Help me to overcome the fear of death by trusting in Him who is my resurrection. Grant me the power of Your Holy Spirit so that I may live by faith in my risen Lord. Make me able to tell the Good News that Jesus brings eternal life to all who put their trust in Him.

AMEN.

Morning breaks upon the tomb;
Jesus scatters all its gloom.
Day of triumph through the skies;
See the glorious Savior rise.

Ye who are of death afraid
Triumph in the scattered shade.
Drive your anxious cares away;
See the place where Jesus lay.

The Lutheran Hymnal 203, st. 1, 2

46

WHEN JESUS SHOWED HIMSELF ALIVE

God bound Himself to us

GOD AT WORK

On Easter afternoon two of Jesus' followers walked along a country road. They were going back home again to Emmaus, a village about 7 miles from Jerusalem.

They talked about Jesus and everything that had happened to Him. Suddenly Jesus Himself joined them. But they didn't recognize Him. He asked them what they were talking about. "Why do you look so gloomy?"

"You must be the only stranger in Jerusalem who doesn't know what happened," the one named Cleopas said. "Haven't you heard about Jesus? He was a mighty Prophet. He was always doing good. He made sick people well. He helped blind people see again. But our high priests and rulers handed Him over to Pilate to be condemned. They crucified Him, and now He is dead."

"We had hoped that He was the Savior," they said. "We thought He would make us a happy nation. But now He has been dead for 3 days. Something strange has happened, though. Just today we heard that some women in Jerusalem said that Jesus

198

is alive. They said that He arose from the grave. Some of our friends went to the tomb. It was empty, but they didn't see Jesus alive. We just don't know what to think!"

"How foolish you are!" the Stranger said. "Why don't you believe what the women said and what was prophesied in times past? Wasn't it God's plan that the promised Messiah would suffer? He took the punishment for people's sins on Himself. He died to take away their sins. After His work as the Savior is finished He will go to His glory with the Father."

Still unrecognized, Jesus explained many other things from the Bible. He told how Moses and the prophets had written about the love of God. He showed how they described God's plan of salvation.

When they came near Emmaus, Jesus acted as if He were going on to another town. "Stay with us!" they invited. "It's getting late." Jesus agreed to come in and eat supper with them.

While they were at the table together, Jesus blessed some bread and gave it to His friends. Then they recognized Him. They knew He was Jesus. But then He disappeared. Now they knew why they had felt so good while He was near them. "Didn't our hearts burn within us?" they said to each other.

Eagerly they left their supper table without finishing. They hurried back to Jerusalem. They told the disciples the good news that they had seen Jesus alive.

A CLOSER LOOK

When Jesus rose from the dead, He accomplished the final act of God's plan of salvation. "This Jesus whom you crucified God raised up. God made Him both Lord and Christ," was the main thought of Peter's Pentecost sermon. Through Jesus' work,

199

sinful people become God's holy people. The risen Jesus rules as Lord over all creation.

TO HELP US REMEMBER

Jesus blessed His disciples. He opened their understanding of the Bible. They felt their hearts were on fire when Jesus taught them. He said:

> "O foolish men, and slow of heart to believe all that the prophets have spoken! Was it not necessary that the Christ should suffer these things and enter into His glory?" And beginning with Moses and all the prophets, He interpreted to them in all the Scriptures the things concerning Himself. *Luke 24:25-27*

Peter said that God makes us altogether new through the resurrection of Christ.

> ✠ Blessed be the God and Father of our Lord Jesus Christ! By His great mercy we have been born anew to a living hope through the resurrection of Jesus Christ from the dead, and to an inheritance which is imperishable, undefiled, and unfading, kept in heaven for you, who by God's power are guarded through faith for a salvation ready to be revealed in the last time. *1 Peter 1:3-5*

In Luther's explanation to the *Second Article* of the Apostles' Creed we confess our faith in the Savior who still lives and rules:

> ### What does this mean?
>
> I believe that Jesus Christ—true God, Son of the Father from eternity, and true man, born of the Virgin Mary—is my Lord. At great cost He has saved and redeemed me, a lost and condemned person. He has freed me from sin, death, and the power of the devil—not with silver or gold, but with His holy and precious blood and His innocent suffering and death. All this He has done that I may be His own, live under Him in His kingdom, and serve Him in everlasting righteousness, innocence, and blessedness, just as He is risen from the dead and lives and rules eternally. This is most certainly true.

WHAT THIS MEANS TO ME

Jesus is the Lord of all. Jesus Christ is my Lord! I don't want anyone else. I don't want Satan or any of his helpers to rule me. For they will lead me to eternal death.

Jesus Christ is my Lord! He died on the cross for my sins. But He rose again from the dead on the third day. He won the war with death. As my Lord He leads me to victory; my death in this world is my entrance into life everlasting. My baptism is my assurance that Jesus is my Lord.

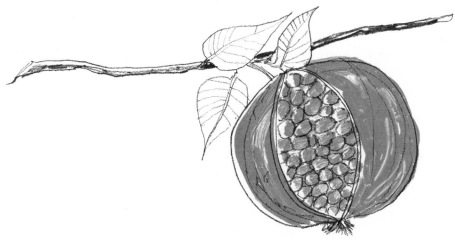

MY PRAYER

Thank You, gracious Father, for conquering death.
Thank You for loving me. Help me to remember
my baptism which gives me the hope of eternal
life. Help me to speak to someone today about
Your great work of rescuing us. Give him eternal
life with You, too, through Jesus, our living
Savior.

AMEN.

"Abide with us, the day is waning,"
Thus prayed the two while on the way;
We read that Thou, O Lord, remaining,
Didst all their doubts and fears allay.
Incline Thine ear, Thou King of Grace,
When, praying thus, we seek Thy face.

When earthly help no more availeth,
To sup with us Thou wilt be nigh;
Thou givest strength that never faileth,
In Thee we grave and death defy.
While earth is fading from our sight,
Our eyes behold the realms of light.

The Lutheran Hymnal 194, st. 1, 5

47

WHEN JESUS ROSE FROM THE DEAD

God gave us the land of heaven

GOD AT WORK

Early Easter evening the disciples of Jesus locked themselves in their room. They were afraid that the enemies of Jesus would arrest them too.

Then, in the wink of an eye, Jesus stood in their midst. He had been there invisibly all the time, of course. Now He just made Himself appear so they could see Him. "Peace be to you," He said.

The disciples were startled. They thought He was a ghost.

"Why are you troubled?" Jesus asked. "Why do you doubt and ask questions? Look at My hands and feet. It is I Myself. Touch Me and see. A spirit does not have flesh and bones as I have."

The disciples were so happy they could hardly believe it! So Jesus asked them, "Do you have anything here to eat?" They gave Him a piece of broiled fish; Jesus ate it.

Then He said to them, "This is what I said to you while I was still with you. All things written about Me in Moses, the Psalms, and the prophets must be fulfilled."

Jesus explained the Scriptures to them. "This is what is written," Jesus said. "The Messiah must die and rise again from the dead on the third day and repentance and forgiveness of sins be preached in His name to all nations. Begin here in Jerusalem. You are witnesses to all of this. I want you to know that I will send My Spirit upon you. So stay here in the city until He gives you power."

203

A CLOSER LOOK

Jesus rose from the dead to show that He is the Son of God with power. All the Old Testament promises find their end in Him. He conquered death and brought us life. Since He is risen from the dead, we also shall rise from the dead.

The Spirit of God begins eternal life in us right now. God began the new age of victory and hope through the resurrection of His Son.

God gets us ready for heaven through the message of the Gospel which brings forgiveness. He keeps us alive in the faith in Jesus. One day He will lead us into the land which He gave us when Jesus died and rose again.

TO HELP US REMEMBER

Jesus is our new beginning: away from sin and death and into life with God. Jesus said:

> ✠ "I am the Resurrection and the Life; he who believes in Me, though he die, yet shall he live, and whoever lives and believes in Me shall never die."   *John 11:25-26a*

Jesus said that believers have eternal life in Him right now.

> ✠ He who believes in the Son has eternal life; he who does not obey the Son shall not see life, but the wrath of God rests upon him.   *John 3:36*

In the *Third Article* we confess our faith in God who gives us heaven through the work of Christ.

> **I believe in the Holy Ghost; the holy Christian church, the communion of saints; the forgiveness of sins; the resurrection of the body; and the life everlasting.**

In his explanation of this article, Martin Luther wrote in part:

> I believe that . . . the Holy Spirit . . . fully forgives my sins and the sins of all believers. On the last day He will raise me and all the dead and give me and all believers in Christ eternal life.

WHAT THIS MEANS TO ME

I am a pilgrim on earth because God has made me a citizen of a new land. I must not live as if the earth were my only home. How much money I have or what I eat and wear are not the important things in life. God grants me many gifts, including food and clothing. But I know that His most important gift to me is eternal life through Christ, my Lord.

In Baptism God began His life in me. In Baptism He buried me with Christ so that my pride, selfishness, jealousy, and love-lessness might be drowned. God makes His Spirit alive in me so that I may love and forgive my neighbor, working to make him happy. My baptism reminds me to repent of my sin and to accept God's grace every day.

By the Word of His grace God keeps me alive in the hope of heaven. Whatever I suffer now is not worth comparing with the joy God has in store for me in heaven.

MY PRAYER

Lord Jesus, accept my praise! You died for me
and now You live forever. Grant me the grace to
believe that Your victory over death is also for
me. Make the hope of heaven strong in me so
that I may live on earth to please You.

AMEN.

Thanks to Thee, O Christ victorious!
Thanks to Thee, O Lord of Life!
Death hath now no power o'er us,
Thou hast conquered in the strife.
Thanks because Thou didst arise
And hast opened Paradise!
None can fully sing the glory
Of the resurrection story.

The Lutheran Hymnal 207, st. 2

48

WHEN JESUS COMMISSIONED HIS DISCIPLES

He commanded them to baptize and teach

GOD AT WORK

The disciples of Jesus were still amazed that He had risen from the dead.

One day some of them were at the Sea of Galilee. Peter said to the others, "I am going out fishing." They said, "We will go with you." So they fished all night, but caught nothing.

In the morning Jesus stood on the beach. No one knew it was Jesus. He called out to them, "Friends, did you catch anything?" When they admitted they had not, Jesus said, "Throw the net out on the right side. You will make a catch." When they did what Jesus said, their net was so full of fish they could not haul it aboard again.

Then John, the disciple whom Jesus loved, recognized Him. "It is the Lord," he said. When Peter heard that, he dived into the sea and swam as fast as he could to the shore. The others followed in the boat, pulling the net full of fish behind them.

"Bring some of your fish," Jesus invited. "Come and have breakfast." The disciples saw that Jesus had already prepared a fire. Some fish and bread were ready to eat.

After breakfast Jesus said to Peter, "Simon, son of John, do you love Me more than anyone else?" "Yes, Lord," he answered. "You know that I love You." "Then feed My lambs," Jesus said.

A second time Jesus asked Peter, "Simon, son of John, do you love Me?" "Yes, Lord, You know I love You," Peter said. "Then look after My young sheep," Jesus told him.

A third time Jesus asked him, "Simon, son of John, do you love Me?" Peter was hurt because Jesus asked him the same question three times. "Lord," he said, "You know everything. You know I love You." Jesus said, "Feed My sheep."

A CLOSER LOOK

After Jesus arose from the dead, He continued to work with His disciples. He planned to send them out into the world as His messengers. They would have to be ready to do this.

He gave them a wonderful act to perform: He told them to baptize in the name of the Father and of the Son and of the Holy

Spirit. He promised forgiveness of sins and life everlasting to everyone who would receive Baptism.

But Jesus also ordered His disciples to teach or "feed" the lambs and sheep of His flocks. He wanted the disciples to teach about the glory and power of God's grace which He gives to every person who is baptized.

This is the work of Jesus' disciples in the church of today. They are to baptize and teach as Jesus commanded.

TO HELP US REMEMBER

Jesus wanted Peter to understand the work He had given His disciples. After He had blessed Peter with a large catch of fish He promised:

> "Do not be afraid; henceforth you will be catching men."
> *Luke 5:10b*

Later, after He arose from the dead,

> ✠ Jesus said to Simon Peter, "Simon, son of John, do you love Me more than these?" He said to Him, "Yes, Lord; You know that I love You." He said to him, "Feed My lambs. . . . Tend My sheep." *John 21:15, 16b*

In these words Jesus tells His disciples what their work is:

> ✠ "Go therefore and make disciples of all nations, baptizing them in the name of the Father and of the Son and of the Holy Spirit, teaching them to observe all that I have commanded you; and lo, I am with you always, to the close of the age." *Matthew 28:19-2*

208

This is the twofold commission to the church: To baptize and to teach.

What is Baptism?
Baptism is not water only, but it is water used together with God's Word and by His command.

WHAT THIS MEANS TO ME

God loves me! He made me sure of this when He baptized me in the name of the Father and of the Son and of the Holy Spirit. God forgives me my sins every day. He even forgives my worst sins. In my baptism, He promises to keep me as His own dear child.

God loves all men! In every age Jesus commands His disciples to baptize all nations, and to teach all nations about the blessings of His grace. My congregation is a group of Jesus' disciples who work together to carry out this command.

I pray that God will help me do my part in His work.

MY PRAYER

Thank You, merciful Savior, for bringing me into Your church through Holy Baptism and the teaching of Your Word. Make me a faithful disciple so that I may bring other disciples to You and Your family of believers. Let my strength for Your work always be in Your love for me and all people.

AMEN.

O Spirit of the Lord, prepare
A sinful world their God to meet;
Breathe Thou abroad like morning air
Till hearts of stone begin to beat.

Baptize the nations; far and nigh
The triumphs of the Cross record;
The name of Jesus glorify
Till every kindred call Him Lord.

The Lutheran Hymnal 504, st.

49

WHEN JESUS ASCENDED INTO HEAVEN

He promised His continual presence

GOD AT WORK

The 40 days after Jesus rose from the dead were exciting days for the disciples. Jesus would suddenly appear in their midst and then just as suddenly disappear again! They did not know when or where to expect Him next. Jesus was teaching them how to get along without His visible presence. Yet He wanted them to be sure that He was alive again after His crucifixion.

One day, on top of a hill, Jesus gave them His farewell talk. "Do not leave Jerusalem," He said, "wait a while for My Father's promise. You heard Me give this promise. You know that John baptized with water. But you will be baptized with the Holy Spirit. He will come in the next few days. When the Holy Spirit comes you will receive power. You will be My witnesses in Jerusalem, all over Judea and Samaria, and all the way to the ends of the earth. And even though you do not see Me, I will be with you all the time."

Then Jesus raised His hands to bless His disciples. While He did this, He slowly rose into the sky. His disciples watched in wonder as they saw Him rise. Soon a cloud covered Him completely. But they still kept looking, perhaps hoping to see Him again.

Acts 1

Jesus did not continue to stay on earth as He did during the 3 years of His ministry. He left to rule the whole world from His throne at the right hand of God. He left so that He could carry out His promise of the coming of the Holy Spirit.

But even though Jesus left, He was still with His disciples. He was with them in the Holy Spirit. The Holy Spirit gave them the power to be His witnesses and power to believe that Jesus was truly present with them.

Jesus is present with His disciples today. He is present also in His Word, in Baptism, and in the Holy Supper. We cannot see Jesus any more than His disciples could see Him after His ascension. But the Holy Spirit gives Jesus' disciples of today the same power He gave the first disciples. Jesus is still ruling the whole world from His throne at the right hand of God.

Jesus wants His disciples of today to be His witnesses everywhere.

211

TO HELP US REMEMBER

We should remember the exact words of Jesus' promise to be with His disciples forever and ever:

> "Lo, I am with you always, to the close of the age."
> *Matthew 28:20b*

Jesus is present with His disciples and lives in them with His Spirit.

> ✠ "You shall receive power when the Holy Spirit has come upon you; and you shall be My witnesses in Jerusalem and in all Judea and Samaria and to the end of the earth."
> *Acts 1:8*

Jesus promised that the Holy Spirit would teach the disciples how to do the work He had commanded them to do.

> ✠ "But the Counselor, the Holy Spirit, whom the Father will send in My name, He will teach you all things, and bring to your remembrance all that I have said to you."
> *John 14:26*

Paul reminds us that we were buried with Christ in Baptism that we might rise to newness of life with Him.

> ✠ If then you have been raised with Christ, seek the things that are above, where Christ is, seated at the right hand of God. Set your minds on things that are above, not on things that are on earth. *Colossians 3:1-2*

In the *Second Article* of the Apostles' Creed we confess:

> **the third day He rose again from the dead; He ascended into heaven and sitteth on the right hand of God the Father Almighty; from thence He shall come to judge the quick and the dead.**

WHAT THIS MEANS TO ME

Sometimes I wish I could see Jesus as the first disciples did. But they too had to learn to live without actually seeing Him. Sometimes I forget that Jesus is really with me. This makes me want to sin. Sin makes me feel afraid.

But Jesus gives me the wonderful promise which He will never break. He promises to be with me all the time. He gives me His Holy Spirit, who makes me able to believe His promises.

By His power I am His witness. I can show that I am His child by what I say and by how I live. I want to share the joyful good news of forgiveness and life everlasting with many other people.

MY PRAYER

> Lord Christ, Ruler of heaven and earth, thank You
> for Your promise to be with Your church. Thank
> You for Your Holy Spirit through whom I have
> come to believe You are present all the time and
> at all places. Help me to obey Your commands
> and to think happily of my new home with You
> in heaven. Make me a joyful witness of Your
> mighty work of redemption.
>
> AMEN.

We thank Thee, Jesus, dearest Friend,
That Thou didst into heaven ascend.
O blessed Savior, bid us live
And strength to soul and body give.
                    Hallelujah!

Ascended to His throne on high,
Hid from our sight, yet always nigh,
He rules and reigns at God's right hand
And has all power at His command.
                    Hallelujah!
The Lutheran Hymnal 223, st. 1, 2

213

50

WHEN JESUS ASCENDED INTO HEAVEN

the angels promised His return

GOD AT WORK

The disciples stood looking at the sky. They could hardly believe what they saw. The Lord Jesus was rising into the sky! Then a cloud removed Him from their sight.

All at once two men in white stood beside them. "Men of Galilee, why stare at the sky?" they asked the disciples. "You can see that Jesus has gone away from you into heaven. He will come again in the same way that you have seen Him go."

Acts 1
Matthew 25

The angels told the disciples *how* He would return to the earth, but they did not tell them *when* He would come.

Jesus at one time had described His second coming. "The Son of Man will come in His glory and all the angels with Him. He will sit on His throne, with all the nations gathered before Him. He will divide people into two groups, like a shepherd separates the sheep from the goats. He will place the sheep at His right and the goats at His left.

"'You have My Father's blessing,' the King will say to those at His right. 'Come and live in the kingdom that has been ready for you since the world was made. I was hungry and you gave Me food. I was thirsty and you gave Me drink. I was a Stranger and you took Me into your home. I was naked and you clothed Me. I was sick and you visited Me. I was in prison and you came to Me.'"

The believers will be surprised to hear the Lord say this to them. Then He will explain: "Anything you did for one of the least of these My brothers, you did for Me."

To those at His left, who chose to live without Him, Jesus will say, "Go from My sight into the eternal fire prepared for the devil and his angels. Anything you did not do for one of the least of these you did not do for Me."

These unbelievers will go to eternal punishment but the believers, clean and renewed through God's forgiveness, will enter eternal life. This will happen when Jesus comes to earth again.

A CLOSER LOOK

The same Jesus who ascended into heaven will come in person to earth again. He will come in glory and honor to raise the dead and gather God's people for eternal life. He is now at

God's right hand, ruling the world; at His second coming He will openly reveal to all that He is Lord indeed.

Will we know Him when He returns? Yes. Everyone will see Him and recognize Him as the Lord. In the meantime we try to help each other on earth. When we show love to others, we show love for Jesus.

TO HELP US REMEMBER

Watch for Jesus' second coming!

✠ "This Jesus, who was taken up from you into heaven, will come in the same way as you saw Him go into heaven."
Acts 1:11

Jesus will rule visibly when He returns again. Let us live to show that we expect our Lord. Peter writes:

✠ Therefore gird up your minds, be sober, set your hope fully upon the grace that is coming to you at the revelation of Jesus Christ. *1 Peter 1:13*

Through Baptism God brought us out from under Satan's power. He moved us into the kingdom of His beloved Son. In the *Seventh Petition* of the Our Father we pray for that day when God will make His gracious rule over us complete by taking us into His heavenly kingdom.

But deliver us from evil.

What does this mean?

We ask in this inclusive prayer that our heavenly Father would save us from every evil to body and soul, and at our last hour would mercifully take us from the troubles of this world to Himself in heaven.

WHAT THIS MEANS TO ME

God has already appointed the day when Christ will return. Since He has not told anyone when it is to be, I live each day trusting His grace to save me. And since the time is short, I must work to spread the Gospel to people everywhere.

Watch and pray! I must be prepared for my Savior's coming and let no other gods tempt me to worship them. I will pray for the Holy Spirit to keep me in the true faith.

Jesus counts works of love as done to Him. I will think of those people who need something from me: love, help, forgiveness, encouragement. Jesus gives me the power to love these people and to look for His return to earth.

MY PRAYER

> O Lord, heavenly Father, stir my heart and mind
> to remember the end of time and Your judgment.
> Make me watchful so that I am not trapped in the
> worship of gods who cannot help me. Preserve
> me by Your mercy so that I may await the Savior's
> coming with joy. By the preaching of Your Word
> prepare the world for His return.
>
> AMEN.

Great God, what do I see and hear?	O Christ, who diedst and yet dost live,
The end of things created;	To me impart Thy merit;
The Judge of mankind doth appear	My pardon seal, my sins forgive,
On clouds of glory seated.	And cleanse me by Thy Spirit.
The trumpet sounds; the graves restore	Beneath Thy cross I view the day
The dead which they contained before.	When heaven and earth shall pass away,
Prepare, my soul, to meet Him.	And thus prepare to meet Thee.

The Lutheran Hymnal 604, st. 1, 4

SECTION SIX GOD'S HOLY SPIRIT
WHO BUILDS CHRIST'S CHURCH

51

WHEN GOD SENT HIS HOLY SPIRIT

He gathered His church together in Christ

GOD AT WORK

It was 10 days since the disciples watched Jesus ascend into heaven. They were waiting in Jerusalem as Jesus had asked them to do. They remembered His promise to send them the Holy Spirit and power. How would God keep His promise? How would the Holy Spirit come to them?

The city of Jerusalem was filled with travelers and strangers from many lands. It was Pentecost, the festival of the seventh Sabbath after the Passover. Thousands of people had come to Jerusalem from all over the world to celebrate this festival.

Then it happened! First there was a noise. It was like a mighty wind blowing down the streets. This loud sound led crowds of people to the house where the disciples were assembled in prayer. Little flames of fire were seen on the people who were present. The disciples began to speak in strange languages! Many people were amazed to hear these Galileans speak.

Simon Peter believed that the Holy Spirit had come. He began to preach about this great miracle.

"Listen to me. These strange things were promised by God through the prophet Joel when He said, 'I will pour out My Spirit upon all flesh . . . [they] shall prophesy. And I will show wonders in the heaven above and signs on the earth beneath.' Jesus of Nazareth performed mighty miracles among you. God did these through Him. You crucified this Jesus, but God raised Him up again. All of us are witnesses to His resurrection. He is now at the right hand of God. Before He ascended, He promised to send us His Holy Spirit. This is the day of the fulfillment of His promise. God has made this Jesus both Lord and Christ."

When the crowd heard Peter's sermon they were cut to the heart. They asked Peter and the apostles, "Brethren, what shall we do?"

Peter replied, "Repent, and be baptized every one of you in the name of Jesus Christ for the forgiveness of your sins; and you shall receive the gift of the Holy Spirit. The promise is to you and your children and to all that are far off—everyone whom the Lord our God calls to Him."

Those who believed Peter's words were baptized. Christ's

church began that day; and about three thousand people were gathered into it by the Spirit. These people continued to worship and pray together and came together regularly to hear the teachings of Christ's apostles.

A CLOSER LOOK

God kept Jesus' promise to send His Holy Spirit to the disciples. Pentecost was the day the Spirit came. Through the Word and Baptism, the Holy Spirit gathers many people into the church of Jesus Christ.

Christ's church is present when people gather regularly to preach and hear the Gospel and to celebrate the sacraments.

TO HELP US REMEMBER

We should try to remember some of the stirring words of the apostle Peter in his Pentecost sermon:

✠ "Repent and be baptized every one of you in the name of Jesus Christ for the forgiveness of your sins; and you shall receive the gift of the Holy Spirit."　　　*Acts 2:38*

On this day God's Holy Spirit gathered thousands of people into Christ's church. These people came together regularly to study and pray.

✠ And they devoted themselves to the apostles' teaching and fellowship, to the breaking of bread and the prayers.
Acts 2:42

In the explanation to the *Third Article* of the Apostles' Creed, Luther describes the work of the Holy Spirit in gathering the church.

I believe that I cannot by my own understanding or effort believe in Jesus Christ, my Lord, or come to Him. But the Holy Spirit has called me through the Gospel, enlightened me with His gifts, and sanctified and kept me in true faith. In the same way He calls, gathers, enlightens, and sanctifies the whole Christian church on earth, and keeps it united with Jesus Christ in the one true faith. In this Christian church day after day He fully forgives my sins and the sins of all believers.

WHAT THIS MEANS TO ME

It's hard for me to understand that I cannot see the church of Christ which the Holy Spirit gathers. I must remember that instead of *seeing* Christ's church, I *believe in* Christ's church. I learn through God's apostles that Christ founded His church. The Day of Pentecost marks its beginning.

Yet I *can* see the gathering of people who praise God together in their hymns and prayers. I can join with these people in their worship of God. I know God's Holy Spirit made me a member of Christ's church by my baptism.

I praise God for adding me to His church. I look forward to being in His heavenly kingdom.

MY PRAYER

Thank you, God, for sending Your Holy Spirit to call me by Baptism into Your holy church. Help me to find joy in worshiping with the people of the church in my own congregation. Make Your church grow with many new members, for the sake of the Head of the church, Jesus Christ.
AMEN.

Let songs of praises fill the sky: Christ, our ascended Lord, Sends down His Spirit from on high According to His Word. All hail the day of Pentecost, The coming of the Holy Ghost!

Come, Holy Spirit, from above With Thy celestial fire; Come and with flames of zeal and love Our hearts and tongues inspire. Be this our day of Pentecost, The coming of the Holy Ghost!

The Lutheran Hymnal 232, st. 1, 4

52

WHEN GOD'S HOLY SPIRIT CAME

He gave His church power

GOD AT WORK

As Peter and John walked into the temple to pray, a lame man begged them for some money.

"I have no money," Peter said. "But I will give you what I do have. In the name of Jesus Christ of Nazareth: walk!" The man jumped up and sang for joy. He was healed.

When he walked into the temple with Peter and John, several people recognized him. They were amazed to see what had happened to him. Peter saw that a crowd was gathering, so he spoke to them.

"Men of Israel, why are you surprised at this? Why stare at us, as if it were our power that made this man walk? The God of our fathers gave the highest honor to His servant, Jesus. But you put Him on trial. When Pilate gave you a choice, you let Barabbas, the murderer, go free. You killed Jesus, the Author of life, whom God raised from the dead. We are witnesses of that. It is Jesus who has made this man strong. The faith which trusts Jesus has given this man perfect health, as you can see for yourselves."

The leaders of the temple didn't want the disciples to preach about Jesus and the resurrection from the dead. They arrested Peter and John and put them in prison over night. The next day the court asked them, "By what power have men like you healed the lame man?"

"It was by the name of Jesus Christ of Nazareth, whom you crucified, whom God raised from the dead," said Peter. "By Him this man stands before you fit and well. There is no sal-

vation in anyone else. For there is no other name under heaven given to men by which we may receive salvation."

When the leaders heard that, the court ordered Peter and John never again to teach in the name of Jesus.

But the disciples replied, "Do you think it is right in God's eyes for us to obey you rather than Him? We can't stop speaking of things we have seen and heard."

After the court released them, the disciples went back to their friends. Together they prayed, "Great God, stretch out Your hand to heal. Help Your servants to speak Your Word boldly. Cause signs and wonders to be done through the name of your holy servant Jesus." When they ended their prayer the building shook. Everyone was filled with the Holy Spirit and boldly spoke the Word of God.

A CLOSER LOOK

The disciples needed a power from outside themselves to bring all nations to Christ. God gave them His power when He sent them His Holy Spirit. Many people heard the disciples tell about Jesus and believed. After the healing of the lame man, the number of believers reached about five thousand.

TO HELP US REMEMBER

The Holy Spirit gave His church special power so that the disciples could heal the lame man and boldly tell others about it. Peter said:

> ✠ "Be it known to you all, and to all the people of Israel, that by the name of Jesus Christ of Nazareth, whom you crucified, whom God raised from the dead, by Him this man is standing before you well. This is the Stone which was rejected by you builders, but which has become the Head of the corner.
>
> And there is salvation in no one else, for there is no other name under heaven given among men by which we must be saved."   *Acts 4:10-12*

God's Spirit works when men proclaim the forgiveness of sins in Christ. This proclamation is called the Gospel. Paul writes:

> ✠ For I am not ashamed of the Gospel: it is the power of God for salvation to every one who has faith, to the Jew first and also to the Greek.   *Romans 1:16*

God puts His power to work in Baptism where He forgives sins and gives eternal life to all who believe. How can water do such great things? Luther answered:

> It is not water that does these things, but God's Word with the water and our trust in this Word. Water by itself is only water, but with the Word of God it is a life-giving water which by grace gives the new birth through the Holy Spirit. St. Paul writes in Titus 3: "He saved us . . . in virtue of His own mercy, by the washing of regeneration and renewal in the Holy Spirit."

WHAT THIS MEANS TO ME

On my own I cannot do God's will. Even if I try, I still do not love God with all my heart, nor do I love my neighbor as myself. Many times I forget that God has made me His child. I need the Holy Spirit's power.

Jesus promised that the Father will give the Holy Spirit to those who ask for Him. In remembering my baptism I have the assurance that the power of God's Spirit is mine, too. God keeps His promise to me. In the Spirit's strength I can fight my sins. I can tell others of God's forgiveness and love.

MY PRAYER

> Almighty, everlasting God, give me Your Holy Spirit. I am weak and powerless to follow Jesus unless You bless me. Make me and Your whole church bold to speak of Your works of grace and love in our blessed Savior.
>
> AMEN.

> Thou holy Fire, Comfort true,
> Grant us the will Thy work to do
> And in Thy service to abide;
> Let trials turn us not aside.
> Lord, by Thy power prepare each heart
> And to our weakness strength impart
> That bravely here we may contend,
> Through life and death to Thee, our Lord, ascend.
> Hallelujah! Hallelujah!
>
> *The Lutheran Hymnal* 224, st. 3

227

53

WHEN JESUS CALLED SAUL

He converted Saul into His apostle

GOD AT WORK

Saul of Tarsus, a Roman citizen, was also a loyal Pharisee. He believed that followers of Jesus rejected the true religion of God. He felt Christians should be punished if they did not return to the temple worship of God. He did not believe Jesus was God's Son. Therefore he agreed with the council which commanded Peter and John to stop talking about Jesus. The officials chose Saul to arrest the people who admitted they were believers in Christ.

Hearing that there were Christians in Damascus, Saul asked permission to visit that city. The officers gave him letters which would tell the leaders in the synagogs there why he had come and that he had permission to arrest any who followed the Christian way of life. If Saul needed to tie them up so they could not escape, he had authority to do that too.

But on the way to Damascus God changed Saul's life. As he neared the city, a bright light from heaven suddenly shone down on him. Falling to the ground, he heard a voice: "Saul, Saul, why do you persecute Me?"

"Tell me, Lord, who are You?" Saul asked.

"I am Jesus, whom you are persecuting. Get up and go into the city and you will be told what to do."

The men who traveled with Saul were surprised and couldn't talk. They heard the voice, but they couldn't see anyone.

Saul got up from the ground and opened his eyes, but he could not see; he was blind. His friends led him by the hand into Damascus. For three days he was blind and didn't eat or drink.

Then God sent a Christian man named Ananias to baptize Saul and heal him. "The Lord Jesus has sent me so that you may regain your sight and be filled with the Holy Spirit," Ananias said to Saul, and he prayed over Saul. Immediately something like scales fell from Saul's eyes and he could see again. He got up, was baptized, ate, and was strengthened.

Later God sent him to many places as "Paul," an apostle of Jesus. God changed Saul, the persecutor, to Paul, the famous missionary.

A CLOSER LOOK

God prepares every disciple of Jesus for His work. First He converts the sinner to faith in Jesus by the power of His Spirit. Then by the same Spirit He equips this disciple for a personal calling. He trains each Christian to witness in his own way for the Lord Jesus.

When God has a certain task to do, He calls and powers a certain disciple to do it. Like Saul every Christian receives Jesus' call to work for Him in an important way.

TO HELP US REMEMBER

The Holy Spirit converts us from sinners to saints. He turns us away from the darkness of sin, the rule of Satan, and the worship of false gods. He brings us to the worship of the true God and Jesus Christ. The prophet Ezekiel describes this work of conversion in the following words of God:

> ✠ "I will give them one heart, and put a new spirit within them; I will take the stony heart out of their flesh and give them a heart of flesh, that they may walk in My statutes and keep My ordinances and obey them; and they shall be My people, and I will be their God." *Ezekiel 11:19-20*

Jesus told Paul that he in turn would help convert others.

> "I send you to open their eyes, that they may turn from darkness to light and from the power of Satan to God, that they may receive forgiveness of sins and a place among those who are sanctified by faith in Me."
> *Acts 26:18*

God sent apostles as gifts to His church. God still sends gifts: pastors and teachers who help believers receive power from God for their work as witnesses. Paul wrote,

> ✠ And His gifts were that some should be apostles, some prophets, some evangelists, some pastors and teachers, for the equipment of the saints, for the work of ministry, for building up the body of Christ. *Ephesians 4:11-12*

This is how we praise God for our own conversion in the words of the explanation to the *Third Article.*

> I believe that I cannot by my own understanding or effort believe in Jesus Christ, my Lord, or come to Him. But the Holy Spirit has called me through the Gospel, enlightened me with His gifts, and sanctified and kept me in true faith.

WHAT THIS MEANS TO ME

How do I know that I am converted? God tells me that He did this wonderful work in me. When I was baptized, God made me His own dear child. He promises to forgive me my sins and keep me as His own forever. I know that I am His.

Every Sunday I want to join my fellow Christians in thanking God for converting me. Every day I pray for His Holy Spirit so that I may always live as His children should. Some day God may call me to be a special minister in His church.

MY PRAYER

> O God, heavenly Father, give me Your Spirit and strengthen my faith. Keep turning me to Yourself so that I may always worship and serve You. By the power of Your Word help me to show others the place You have for them in Your kingdom; through the faith in Jesus that Your Holy Spirit works in them.
>
> AMEN.

It is Thy work alone
That I am now converted;
O'er Satan's work in me
Thou hast Thy power asserted.
Thy mercy and Thy grace
That rise afresh each morn
Have turned my stony heart
Into a heart new-born.

The Lutheran Hymnal 417, st. 2

54

WHEN JESUS COMMISSIONED PAUL

He showed a special concern for the Gentiles

GOD AT WORK

God made Paul His special apostle to the Gentiles.

Enemies of Jesus wanted to kill Paul. They said that he destroyed the true religion of Israel and started fights among the people. They arrested him. They took him to court in Jerusalem and in Caesarea. Then Paul demanded a trial in Rome. Since he was a Roman citizen, they had to take him to Rome.

The soldiers guarded Paul on his long and exciting sea voyage to Rome. When they arrived, instead of being imprisoned, Paul was allowed to stay with the one soldier who guarded him. So God gave him the opportunity to continue His witness to Jesus.

Soon after he arrived he invited the religious leaders to visit him. He told them how he happened to be a prisoner of the Romans. He said that fellow Israelites wanted to punish him for preaching about Jesus. He had asked for his trial to be held in Rome. The leaders told Paul, "We have received no letters from Judea about you. No one who has moved here lately has said anything against you. We would like to hear what you have to say. We know that everyone is talking about this group called 'Christians.'" They agreed on a day when they could talk over the matter.

232

On the chosen day a large crowd came to Paul's house. He taught them. He told them of the kingdom of God, trying to convince them that Jesus is the promised Messiah. He showed them how Moses and the prophets spoke of Jesus as the coming Savior. Some were convinced by what he said. Others did not believe him.

Because some of the Israelites did not believe, Paul made one last statement before they left. "The Holy Spirit was right when He spoke to your fathers through the prophet Isaiah, 'This people's heart has grown dull. Their ears are hard of hearing. They have closed their eyes. They will not turn to Me to heal them.' You can be certain that God has sent this salvation to the Gentiles. They will listen."

Paul lived in Rome two years. He welcomed all who came to him. He preached the coming of the kingdom of God through faith in the Lord Jesus Christ. He said the Kingdom comes to everyone who believes: Jew and Gentile, slave and free, men and women.

A CLOSER LOOK

God made known His concern also for the Gentiles at Rome through the apostle Paul. He had first made His covenant of mercy and forgiveness with the people of Israel. Gentiles were people from other nations. God's mercy was also for them. Israel was to bear the news of God's love to all nations. But when many of the Israelites rejected Jesus, they rejected God's offer of life through Him. Then God said He would bring His salvation to the Gentiles—*without* Israel's help! All those from Israel who refused God's mercy in Jesus were not really God's people at all.

TO HELP US REMEMBER

God calls people everywhere to life in Jesus. Israel already had received the message of God's forgiveness in Jesus. Now Paul said to them:

> ✠ "Let it be known to you then that this salvation of God has been sent to the Gentiles; they will listen."
>
> *Acts 28:28*

Isaiah had promised that God's servant, Jesus, would be a "Light to the nations."

> ✠ "I am the Lord, I have called You in righteousness, I have taken You by the hand and kept You; I have given You as a covenant to the people, a Light to the nations."
>
> *Isaiah 42:6*

When Paul preached in Antioch of Pisidia, he told the people there that Jesus is the Light of the world.

> "For so the Lord has commanded us, saying, 'I have set You to be a light for the Gentiles, that You may bring salvation to the uttermost parts of the earth.'" And when the Gentiles heard this, they were glad and glorified the Word of God.
>
> *Acts 13:47-48a*

In the *Third Article* we say that we believe in "the holy Christian church, the communion of saints." That means we believe that the Holy Spirit works through His Word to gather Christians from every nation and tongue on earth.

> In the same way He calls, gathers, enlightens, and sanctifies the whole Christian church on earth, and keeps it united with Jesus Christ in the one true faith.

WHAT THIS MEANS TO ME

The words of St. Paul to the people of Israel when they rejected Jesus are a warning for me. God called Israel His people, but when they disobeyed Him and denied Jesus, they were no longer His spiritual people.

I am one of God's people. He made His covenant with me in my baptism. But I have this promise only by His grace and mercy; I did not deserve this honor. God's grace goes out through me when I take an active part in spreading the good news of forgiveness to every land.

MY PRAYER

Light of the nations, Savior of all men, Thank You for bringing me into Your kingdom of life. Remove all pride from my heart. Keep me from deceiving myself into thinking that it is my good works which earn Your favor. Give me grace to repent of my sin and look to Your mercy. Help me to tell others of the goodness of that mercy.
AMEN.

Can we whose souls are lighted
With wisdom from on high,
Can we to men benighted
The lamp of life deny?
Salvation! Oh, Salvation!
The joyful sound proclaim
Till each remotest nation
Has learned Messiah's name.

The Lutheran Hymnal 495, st. 3

235

55

WHEN GOD SENT HIS HOLY SPIRIT

He used the apostles to reveal many truths

GOD AT WORK

One day Paul heard some bad news about his friends in Galatia. False teachers were trying to lead them away from Jesus. Some of the men and women whom Paul himself had taught seemed to be ready to believe the false teachings.

The men who tried to mislead the Christians were called Judaizers. They taught that people are safer in their faith if they obey the Old Testament laws. "What really makes a person a child of God is to obey each detail of the law of Israel," they said.

Paul worried about his friends in Galatia. But what could he do to help them? He was so far away. He decided to write them a letter. God's Holy Spirit moved Paul so that what he wrote was God's own work. His letter would help his friends to know Jesus and to follow Him in love.

"I am astonished!" Paul wrote, "that you are so quickly deserting Him who called you in the grace of Christ. You are turning to a different gospel, which is no Gospel at all. The trouble

236

is with the people who want to mislead you. They try to change the Gospel of Christ. No one, not we nor even an angel from heaven, should preach a gospel different from that which we already gave you. If anyone does, let him be cursed."

Paul showed that God saves sinners only through faith in Jesus. This message comes from Jesus Himself; no one made it up! Paul said that his own life was a good example of how God saves people through faith in Jesus alone. "God called me through His grace," Paul said. "He chose to reveal His Son to me and through me so that I might proclaim Him among the Gentiles."

"Christ set us free," Paul wrote. "Stand firm, then, and refuse to be slaves to sin again. Use your freedom in Christ as the opportunity to love one another."

Paul wrote letters to other Christians in different places, where he had organized Christian congregations. The New Testament Scriptures also contain letters written by other apostles, such as James, Peter, John, and Jude.

A CLOSER LOOK

The apostles and evangelists spoke and wrote as God's messengers. What they wrote by God's will has been collected and forms the New Testament of the Holy Scriptures. In these books and letters God shows how Jesus fulfilled all that was promised. He is the Messiah whom God said would come to save His people from their sins. The witness of the apostles in the New Testament is that God spoke His complete and final Word to men in His own Son, Jesus Christ.

237

TO HELP US REMEMBER

God called some of the men who had seen Jesus to write a witness to Him. Peter describes the work of the Holy Spirit in these apostles by the following words:

> ✠ First of all you must understand this, that no prophecy of Scripture is a matter of one's own interpretation, because no prophecy ever came by the impulse of man, but men moved by the Holy Spirit spoke from God.
>
> *2 Peter 1:20-21*

Paul wrote to Timothy:

> ✠ All Scripture is inspired by God. *2 Timothy 3:16a*

We call the writers of the Gospels the evangelists. We can group all the books of the New Testament under three headings: history, epistles, and prophecy.

HISTORY	EPISTLES		PROPHECY
Matthew	Romans	Titus	Revelation
Mark	1, 2 Corinthians	Philemon	
Luke	Galatians	Hebrews	
John	Ephesians	James	
The Acts	Philippians	1, 2 Peter	
	Colossians	1, 2, 3 John	
	1, 2 Thessalonians	Jude	
	1, 2 Timothy		

238

WHAT THIS MEANS TO ME

I praise God for revealing Himself to me! I believe that the Holy Spirit moved the apostles of the New Testament to write His Word. I believe that the Holy Spirit strengthens my faith as I read and study these holy writings.

When I read the New Testament I am moved to thank God for fulfilling His promise of salvation for sinners. I can see that Jesus is the fulfillment of these promises made in Old Testament days.

I pray that God's Spirit may deepen my love for the Holy Scriptures so that I take every opportunity to use them in my life.

MY PRAYER

> Send me Your Spirit, gracious Father, so that I may receive Jesus, Your living Word. Thank You for the gift of the New Testament in which Your apostles reveal Him to me. Help me to know my Bible, so that I may know You and Jesus Christ whom You have sent. Give me grace to love and serve Him in the fellowship of His church.
>
> AMEN.

> God's Word is our great heritage
> And shall be ours forever;
> To spread its light from age to age
> Shall be our chief endeavor.
> Through life it guides our way,
> In death it is our stay.
> Lord, grant, while worlds endure,
> We keep its teachings pure
> Throughout all generations.
>
> *The Lutheran Hymnal* 283

239

56

WHEN JESUS CALLS ME
BY HIS HOLY SPIRIT

I become His own, together with all the saints

GOD AT WORK

Let's look back. What a thrilling story we have studied! This has been the history of God's plan of salvation for sinful people. It is the story of the mighty and gracious God at work. It tells how God rescued sinners from everlasting death and gave them everlasting life. It is an unfinished history, for it includes us today.

It all began when God chose Abraham to be the father of many nations — but particularly the father of the people to whom God would give His special love. "For you are a people holy to the Lord your God; the Lord your God has chosen you to be a people for His own possession, out of all the people that are on the face of the earth . . . it is because the Lord loves you, and is keeping the oath which He swore to your fathers, that the Lord has brought you out with a mighty hand . . . the Lord your God is God, the faithful God who keeps covenant and steadfast love with those who love Him and keep His commandments."(Deuteronomy 7:6, 8-9)

But God's people, Israel, sinned and disobeyed. God took them from their land into exile. Yet His steadfast love watched carefully over the remnant of His people who believed. He sent His prophets to proclaim His new covenant to them. Finally, from this remnant of the true people God brought His only-begotten Son.

Jesus born of Mary is the long-promised Messiah, the Second Adam. Jesus, the Man, in His life on earth displayed the power of almighty God. He healed the sick, gave sight to the blind, raised the dead, and proclaimed the Gospel of peace. He conquered all man's enemies: sin, Satan, and death. He fulfilled

240

all the prophecies given in the Old Testament about the Messiah. He kept God's law perfectly. He was obedient even to death. He is the Lamb of God that takes away the sin of the world. In Jesus' resurrection, God completed His work, His plan of salvation. One great event is still to come. Jesus will return in glory to judge the living and the dead.

Before He ascended into heaven, Jesus gathered His disciples. He taught them how to witness to His Word and work. He told them to make disciples of all nations. He gave them the sacraments of Baptism and Holy Communion to help carry out this work. Christ founded the church when He gathered all who trusted Him for salvation.

In Holy Baptism, which Jesus instituted, He calls sinners into His kingdom today. Peter told the believers of his time: "You are a chosen race, a royal priesthood, a holy nation, God's own people, that you may declare the wonderful deeds of Him who called you out of darkness into His marvelous light" (1 Peter 2:9). These words tell us today that we are His new people in the world. All disciples of Jesus Christ form the community of the church: people who glorify and praise God as they speak the word of God's forgiveness to each other and to the world.

This is our call today: to continue to make disciples of all nations and to proclaim the good news of God's great work of salvation in Jesus Christ. Because our heavenly Father has loved us, we can't help but show this love for all our fellowmen in words and in deeds. In this way God's Holy Spirit is at work in today's world through us who are His church.

241

A CLOSER LOOK

See how the time line which started with God's creative act has progressed to the day in which we live? The line will come to an end on the day when Jesus Christ returns to judge the world.

TO HELP US REMEMBER

We want to remember forever Peter's stirring words describing our call:

> ✠ You are a chosen race, a royal priesthood, a holy nation, God's own people, that you may declare the wonderful deeds of Him who called you out of darkness into His marvelous light.
> *1 Peter 2:9*

Peter also writes how Holy Baptism is God's means of calling us and saving us.

> Baptism . . . now saves you, not as a removal of dirt from the body but as an appeal to God for a clear conscience, through the resurrection of Jesus Christ.
> *1 Peter 3:21*

God's new people make up the family which is the church. St. Paul describes the church as a beautiful building in his Letter to the Ephesians:

> ✠ You are fellow citizens with the saints and members of the household of God, built upon the foundation of the apostles and prophets, Christ Jesus Himself being the chief Cornerstone, in whom the whole structure is joined together and grows into a holy temple in the Lord; in whom you also are built into it for a dwelling place of God in the Spirit.
> *Ephesians 2:19-22*

WHAT THIS MEANS TO ME

I have found my place on the time line of the history of God at work. How wonderful it is to be a person whom the almighty God loves! It is the greatest honor for me to be a member of God's chosen people.

I have many lessons to learn from God's people of old. I do not want to become proud and believe that God chose me because I was so good. I do not want to despise His blessings by being disobedient to His commands and will. Yet, even though I sin, when I repent God forgives me all my sins. And He promises to keep me in His kingdom forever.

How happy I am that by the Holy Spirit I am able to tell others of this work of my gracious God in Christ!

MY PRAYER

I praise You, O God, for calling me into Your church. Give me Your Holy Spirit that I may always be the person You want me to be, for Jesus' sake.

AMEN.

The saints on earth and those above
But one communion make;
Joined to their Lord in bonds of love,
All of His grace partake.

One family, we dwell in Him,
One church above, beneath;
Though now divided by the stream,
The narrow stream, of death.

The Lutheran Hymnal 478, st. 1, 2

243

SECTION SEVEN **I PRAISE GOD FOR HIS PLAN**

OF SALVATION

57. I PRAISE GOD
   for giving me His law

58. I PRAISE GOD
   for giving me my faith

59. I PRAISE GOD
   for giving me the privilege of prayer

60. I PRAISE GOD
   for making me His child through Baptism

61. I PRAISE GOD
   for binding Himself to me in His Holy Supper

62. I PRAISE GOD
   for making me His living epistle

57

I PRAISE GOD

for giving me His law

GOD AT WORK

"Which commandment is the first of all?" asked a scribe of Jesus.

"The first is, 'Hear, O Israel: the Lord our God, the Lord is one; and you shall love the Lord your God with all your heart, and with all your soul, and with all your mind, and with all your strength.' The second is this, 'You shall love your neighbor as yourself.' There is no other commandment greater than these." The reply our Lord gave to the question shows that the reason for our obedience is love to God above all people and things.

When God created man (see 5–7), He made man in His own image. This meant that Adam and Eve knew God; they knew God's law perfectly and could obey it perfectly. They praised

God as the Creator. They lived in perfect communion with God. But one day they made the wrong choice (see 8, 9) and tried to be gods themselves. God sent them out of the Garden of Eden. After that their work and pain always reminded them that they had disobeyed God. They could no longer keep His law, for now they and their descendants were sinful.

When God chose the people of Israel, He promised to be their God. "I am the Lord your God, who brought you out of the land of Egypt, out of the house of bondage," proclaimed God, as He revealed His will to His people (see 18, 19). God gave His law to them so that they would know how to keep pure as His people. He promised them victory if they obeyed, and sorrow and trouble if they disobeyed. The story of God's people is one of success and failure. God gave them their land (see 20), and He came to them in their new temple (see 23). But they broke His law continually (see 24). The kingdom of God's people was divided. They followed after false gods. God sent His prophets to warn them of God's anger (see 25). But finally God's patience came to an end. He punished His people by permitting other nations to take them into exile and slavery (see 26). But God's mercy overruled His wrath. He saved a remnant of His people (see 27). From this small group of the true Israel the Son of God was born into the world.

When Jesus preached and taught, He showed God's law and will to all men. He explained the Ten Commandments and showed that in the new covenant days God now demanded more than just knowing and keeping the words of the Law (see 31). When the scribe asked which was the greatest commandment, Jesus pointed out that the Law can be summed up in the one word "love." God asks for love to Himself and to our neighbors. The Ten Commandments show us the blessings which God wants to protect for us.

How many people are able to keep God's law perfectly? Not a single person. And disobedience is sin. Therefore God's law condemns us all because we all have sinned. This is one of the purposes of God's law, to show man his sins. All who belong to God through their baptismal covenant are dismayed by what they see when they look into the mirror of God's law. But the grace of God in the Gospel brings them forgiveness for all their sins against God's law. The Law drives the penitent sinner to the cross of Jesus where God's plan of redemption was completed for their personal salvation.

The Law cannot help us do what it demands. It can only condemn. But God's Word of forgiveness in the Gospel puts love into a sinner's heart and life. By the power of the Spirit we can love God with all our heart and our neighbor as ourselves.

TO HELP US REMEMBER

We should remember the Ten Commandments as God once gave them to His people through Moses. We should remember the explanations which Martin Luther wrote for the commandments. Especially do we wish to remember what God says about His commandments.

What does God say of all these Commandments?

He says: "I, the Lord your God, am a jealous God, visiting the iniquity of the fathers upon the children to the third and fourth generation of those who hate Me, but showing steadfast love to thousands of those who love Me and keep My commandments."

What does this mean for us?

God warns that He will punish all who break these commandments; therefore we are to fear His wrath and not disobey Him. But He promises grace and every blessing to all who keep these commandments; therefore we are to love and trust Him, and gladly do what He commands.

Here are the words of the Lord Jesus as He summarized the law of God in His answer to the scribe:

✠ "'Hear, O Israel: The Lord our God, the Lord is one; and you shall love the Lord your God with all your heart, and with all your soul, and with all your mind, and with all your strength.' . . . 'You shall love your neighbor as yourself.'"

Mark 12:29-31a

WHAT THIS MEANS TO ME

I praise God for giving me His law. It's hard for me to understand how God's law can be a blessing to me. For the Law frightens me when it shows me God's anger because of my many sins. It threatens and condemns me. It demands and forbids things in my life.

Yet it *is* a blessing for me. The Law makes my baptism real to me as it shows me how much I need the forgiveness of God in Jesus. My baptism reminds me to repent of my sins every day and that God has forgiven me my sin. Now I can love in a way that the Law could never force or enable me to love. The Gospel brings the power of the Holy Spirit into my life to help me live God's will.

I also see God's law as a blessing, for it protects the gifts which God has given to mankind. Because of God's law, we can live an orderly and safe life.

I praise God for giving me His law. I praise Him for making me His child.

MY PRAYER

Forgive me all my sins, O heavenly Father. I have
rebelled against Your law. I have so often
forgotten that I am Your child. For Jesus' sake
give me the power of the Holy Spirit so that I may
live a life that is happy in my obedience to Your
law.

AMEN.

Before Jehovah's aweful throne,
Ye nations, bow with sacred joy.
Know that the Lord is God alone;
He can create and He destroy.

We are His people, we His care,
Our souls and all our mortal frame.
What lasting honors shall we rear,
Almighty Maker, to Thy name?

We'll crowd Thy gates with thankful songs,
High as the heavens our voices raise;
And earth, with her ten thousand tongues,
Shall fill Thy courts with sounding praise.

The Lutheran Hymnal 13, st. 1, 3, 4

249

58

I PRAISE GOD

for giving me my faith

GOD AT WORK

"No one has ever seen God," wrote the evangelist St. John; "the only Son, who is in the bosom of the Father, He has made Him known," John continued. This is how John introduced the story of God's work in Christ in his Gospel book.

No one has seen God, yet one can believe in God. God's Holy Spirit gives a person the faith by which he can know God. The Holy Scriptures record all the mighty acts of God by which He makes Himself known to man and brings man to faith in Him.

God is too great for us to describe or to understand. But in faith we can know God from His wonderful works in the world. St. John reminds us that believers know God especially through the living Word who is Jesus Christ our Lord.

All Christians share this faith as members of Christ's church. When Christians confess their faith in the words of the Apostles' Creed, they speak a hymn of praise and worship to God.

"Bless God the Father for His mighty acts!" Christians say. In the beginning God began creating by the power of His Word (see 5).

He made the world and everything in it. He created the first human beings (see 6). He gave them the power to help in His creation. Adam and Eve had children. God made people able to talk with Him. That's what made people different from everything else God created (see 7). God still preserves His world through the power of His Word. He richly and daily provides man with his necessities for life.

"Bless Jesus, God's Son, for His works to save us!" Christians say. Jesus revealed Himself as God's new Champion when He robbed Satan of his power (see 30). Through faith in Jesus believers in every age may overcome the Evil One. When Jesus preached and taught, He revealed God's will for people everywhere (see 31). In His transfiguration He was glorified to show Himself as God's Son (see 35). He suffered in the Garden of Gethsemane and on the cross as the promised Servant of God (see 41—43). He rescued us from our enemies: Satan, sin, and death. When He rose again from the dead, He gave us a new beginning and eternal life in heaven (see 45—47). After He rose from the dead, He commissioned His disciples and then ascended to heaven. On the Last Day He will come to earth again (see 50). He will bring His church into the presence of His Father in heavenly glory.

"Bless God the Holy Spirit who works to purify His people!" Christians say. The Holy Spirit called the church together in Christ on Pentecost (see 51). He fulfilled the promise of the Savior that the Holy Spirit would lead people into the truth (see 49). He gave Jesus' disciples the power to preach the name of Jesus boldly (see 52). He sends pastors and teachers today to help people grow in faith and serve Him (see 53). Through Word and Sacrament—His means of grace—the Holy Spirit keeps His people in the faith which He created in them.

TO HELP US REMEMBER

The Apostles' Creed is an old confession of faith. We easily remember these words since we speak them often in our worship services. Martin Luther wrote a beautiful explanation for each of the three articles of the Creed. We should try to remember these words of his catechism. They help us speak our words of praise to God with more understanding.

St. Paul, writing to the Romans, talked about faith and how to confess it.

> If you confess with your lips that Jesus is Lord and believe in your heart that God raised Him from the dead, you will be saved. For man believes with his heart and so is justified, and he confesses with his lips and so is saved.
>
> *Romans 10:9-10*

In the Creed we confess our faith in the Triune God. Saint Paul expresses the truth of the Trinity in the words of his benediction:

> ✠ The grace of the Lord Jesus Christ and the love of God and the fellowship of the Holy Spirit be with you all.
>
> *2 Corinthians 13:14*

WHAT THIS MEANS TO ME

I praise God for giving me my faith! When He made me His child in Baptism, He gave me the power to believe in Him. My faith helps me to see God in His many acts about me and for me. By faith I know God the Father as my Creator and Protector. By faith I know Jesus as His only Son and my Lord and King. He redeemed me from all my sins. By faith I know God's Holy Spirit who helps me to live a holy life and keeps me in Christ's church. I am one of God's children. He will keep me as His own forever.

I praise God for giving me the opportunity to confess my faith in Him with my fellow members of His church. It is an important moment for me when I join with other Christians in speaking these words of confession. I realize that millions of people have used these same words of praise to God. I pray God for the power to make a continual witness to my Lord in my daily life.

MY PRAYER

Glory be to the Father, and to the Son, and to the Holy Spirit! O mighty God, keep me believing in You until my end. Help me draw many more to You by my confession of faith. In the name of Jesus, the Lord of the church.

AMEN.

We all believe in one true God,
Father, Son, and Holy Ghost,
Ever-present Help in need,
Praised by all the heavenly host,
By whose mighty power alone
All is made and wrought and done.

We all believe in Jesus Christ,
Son of God and Mary's Son,
Who descended from His throne
And for us salvation won;
By whose cross and death are we
Rescued from all misery.

We all confess the Holy Ghost,
Who from both fore'er proceeds;
Who upholds and comforts us
In all trials, fears, and needs.
Blest and holy Trinity,
Praise forever be to Thee!

The Lutheran Hymnal 252

59

I PRAISE GOD

for giving me the privilege of prayer

GOD AT WORK

"O come, let us worship and bow down; let us kneel before the Lord, our Maker! For He is our God, and we are the people of His pasture and the sheep of His hand." (Psalm 95:6-7)

These words come from the prayer book of the Old Testament people, the Psalms. God's devout children spoke and sang these words as they obeyed His command and invitation to call upon Him. They believed God's promise spoken by Isaiah:

"Before they call I will answer; while they are yet speaking I will hear." (Isaiah 65:24)

God created people able to talk with Him (see 7). When man's disobedience destroyed this wonderful fellowship which God had created, God carried out His plan of redemption. He sent His only-begotten Son to pay the price of sin and to reconcile man to God. In His grace and mercy God invites His people to approach Him in prayer and promises to hear their prayers.

When Jesus was on this earth, He taught His disciples how to pray. He gave them the words of a perfect prayer (see 32). He Himself prayed to the heavenly Father (see 40). But above all, Jesus makes it possible for sinful people to talk to God in prayer. Through Jesus sinners have the privilege of calling God Father.

Jesus concluded His lesson on how to pray with these words:

"I tell you, ask, and it will be given you; seek, and you will find; knock, and it will be opened to you" (Luke 11:9). Here Jesus makes the promise to His disciples that God will hear

all their prayers and will answer them according to His wisdom.

God has the power to answer all our prayers. In the Apostles' Creed we call God "Almighty, Maker of heaven and earth" (see 5, 6). Jesus showed God's power in His mighty acts of healing and raising the dead (see 33, 34). So no prayer is too difficult for our heavenly Father to answer. When Jesus rose from the dead, God put an everlasting seal on His promise to hear and answer our prayers. (See 46)

But Jesus taught us that a true prayer is one which looks to God for *His* will (see 41). We must listen to God and not only talk to Him. It is God's will that we forgive our fellowman as we ask God to forgive us. (See 38)

Jesus taught believers to think of each other in their prayers instead of being selfish. Jesus' prayer reads: "*Our* Father . . . give *us* this day *our* daily bread . . . forgive *us our* trespasses as *we* forgive those who trespass against *us* . . . lead *us* not into temptation but deliver *us* from evil" (see 32). When we pray Jesus' prayer, we come to God's throne as a family of believers thinking about each other's needs.

255

Martin Luther wrote a helpful explanation for each of the petitions of the Lord's Prayer. We will want to learn these explanations so that this beautiful prayer can become more meaningful to us. Here are his explanations to the introduction and conclusion of the "Our Father."

The Introduction

Our Father who art in heaven.

What does this mean?

Here God encourages us to believe that He is truly our Father and we are His children. We therefore are to pray to Him with complete confidence just as children speak to their loving father.

The Doxology

For Thine is the kingdom and the power and the glory forever and ever. Amen.

What does "Amen" mean?

Amen means *Yes, it shall be so.* We say *Amen* because we are certain that such petitions are pleasing to our Father in heaven and are heard by Him. For He Himself has commanded us to pray in this way and has promised to hear us.

This psalm verse is a call to worship God.

✠ O come, let us worship and bow down; let us kneel before the Lord, our Maker! For He is our God, and we are the people of His pasture and the sheep of His hand.

Psalm 95:6-7

Jesus' words are a great comfort to us:

✠ "I tell you, Ask, and it will be given you; seek, and you will find; knock, and it will be opened to you." *Luke 11:9*

WHAT THIS MEANS TO ME

I praise God for giving me the privilege of prayer! What a comfort it is to know that I am never alone. When I am in trouble, I can take this trouble to God. When I feel the guilt of my sins pressing upon me, I can confess them to my heavenly Father. I know that for Jesus' sake He will forgive me my sins.

He will hear my call for help and answer me according to His wisdom and grace.

I have so many things for which to be thankful to God! I should begin every day with a word of thanks to God for His goodness to me.

I think of others in my prayers. As a sinner I am tempted to keep on asking for things for myself. Sometimes I even thoughtlessly ask for things which might be hurtful to other people. In praising God I ask Him to make me thoughtful of my fellowmen. I pray for those who are in serious troubles. I pray for those who are lonely and sad. I pray for the many souls who have not learned to know my heavenly Father in Jesus Christ. I pray for the members of my family, for the rulers of my country, and for the leaders of my church and school.

MY PRAYER

Heavenly Father, thank You for the gift of the Holy Spirit who helps me to speak to You in prayer. Thank You for Jesus in whose name I have the privilege of calling You Father. Make my heart thankful always. Widen my circle of interest in others that my prayers may never be selfish but may show the spirit of Jesus' love and sacrifice.

AMEN.

Approach, my soul, the mercy seat
Where Jesus answers prayer;
There humbly fall before His feet,
For none can perish there.

Thy promise is my only plea,
With this I venture nigh;
Thou callest burdened souls to Thee,
And such, O Lord, am I.

The Lutheran Hymnal 456, st. 1, 2

60

I PRAISE GOD

for making me His child through Baptism

GOD AT WORK

A long, long time ago God spoke these terrible words: "I will blot out man whom I have created from the face of the ground, man and beast and creeping things and birds of the air, for I am sorry that I have made them" (Genesis 6:7). Man did not live up to God's plan for him. Man became so disobedient that God decided to destroy him and all creatures.

The Holy Scripture relates how God destroyed man by sending the great flood. All men and creatures were drowned in this flood. Yet God showed mercy by choosing to save Noah and his family (see 11). The water which destroyed men held up the ark in which God saved Noah and his family.

The apostle Peter wrote about this event many years later in his letter to some of the Christians of his time: ". . . when God's patience waited in the days of Noah, during the building

of the ark, in which a few, that is, eight persons, were saved through water. Baptism, which corresponds to this, now saves you . . . as an appeal to God for a clear conscience, through the resurrection of Jesus Christ" (1 Peter 3:20-21). Peter here compares the water of the Flood to the water of Holy Baptism.

Jesus made ordinary water a special blessing when used with His word of grace and promise (see 48). He told His disciples to baptize all nations in "the name of the Father and of the Son and of the Holy Spirit." He promised: "He that believes and is baptized shall be saved." St. Paul called the water of this baptism "the washing of regeneration and renewal in the Holy Spirit, which He poured out upon us richly through Jesus Christ our Savior."

Jesus' command to His disciples to baptize all nations still stands today. God makes us His own children through this sacrament (see 2). God has not removed His power from this sacred act since the time that He instituted it. He who had the power to raise people from the dead (see 34), also had power to raise Himself from the dead (see 45—47). This Lord has the power to give spiritual life to those who are dead in sin. He does this through His Word and Baptism.

259

St. Paul explains this in the words: "All of us who have been baptized into Christ Jesus were baptized into His death . . . we were buried therefore with Him by Baptism into death, so that as Christ was raised from the dead by the glory of the Father, we too might walk in newness of life." This is the daily importance of Baptism for the child of God. It reminds him every day that God has made him His own dear child. By our daily repentance and sorrow for sin we can drown our sinful self as if it were in water. By the power of the Holy Spirit we arise as a new person with power from God to live according to His will. This is how God makes and keeps people His own.

TO HELP US REMEMBER

Martin Luther described the Sacrament of Holy Baptism by asking and answering four questions: What is Baptism? What does Baptism give or profit? How can water do such great things? What does such baptizing with water signify? We want to remember the way he answers these four questions in his catechism. He also gives us the appropriate parts of Holy Scripture which record the work of God in making Baptism His gracious water of life.

We may also remember the summary statement of St. Paul about Baptism:

> For in Christ Jesus you are all sons of God through faith.
> For as many of you as were baptized into Christ have put
> on Christ.   *Galatians 3:26-27*

WHAT THIS MEANS TO ME

I praise God for making me His child through Baptism! Because of the sinfulness of my parents, I was born into this world as a child of the devil. I was born with the desire to rebel against God. I was born to be separated from God forever.

But God rescued me from the power of sin, the devil, and death. My Lord Jesus conquered all these enemies. He offers me forgiveness of sin and thus eternal life. He makes a covenant with me in my baptism that He will do all that He has promised me. I can trust Him and His Word of promise always.

This is the wonderful thought I can have every morning as soon as I wake up: God is my Father, Jesus is my Savior, and God's Spirit gives me power to live as a child of God. When I remember my baptism each day can be a new experience in the grace and love of God.

Jesus wants all nations to become God's children through Baptism. As I live the life of a child of God, I want to join my fellow Christians in the work of witnessing to the love of God so that they too might be brought into His family.

MY PRAYER

O God, I do not deserve Your great goodness to me, for I sin much every day. But I pray, for Jesus' sake forgive me my sins. Forgive me especially for the times that I forget my baptism which made me Your child. By Your Holy Spirit, give me the opportunity to bring others to Your holy family in Christ, our Lord.

AMEN.

He that believes and is baptized
Shall see the Lord's salvation;
Baptized into the death of Christ,
He is a new creation.

Through Christ's redemption he shall stand
Among the glorious heavenly band
Of every tribe and nation.

The Lutheran Hymnal 301, st. 1

261

61

I PRAISE GOD

for binding Himself to me in His Holy Supper

GOD AT WORK

God knows how hard it is for people like us to understand spiritual things. So He uses earthly things to bring His heavenly blessings to men.

A long time ago God's people of the Old Testament had a hard time believing that God would free them from their slavery. To help them see His love for them in His mighty acts, God commanded them to do certain things. When the time had finally come for His people to leave their slavery in Egypt, God described the sacred meal He wanted them to eat on the night of their exodus. They were to kill and eat a special lamb. The blood of this lamb was to be sprinkled on their doorposts. That night the angel of death would come to Egypt to kill the first-born of every family. But the angel would pass over the houses where the blood was on the doorposts. (See 16)

Hundreds of years later, when Jesus walked this earth, He also ate this sacred Passover meal which God had given to His people of old. It was on the night in which He was betrayed (see 39). With the bread and wine which was on the supper table Jesus instituted another holy meal. He took the bread, gave thanks, broke it, and handed it to all the disciples with the words, "Take eat, this is My body which is given for you." Then He took the cup of wine, gave thanks, and gave it to all the disciples, saying, "This cup is the new covenant in My blood."

Jesus is our Passover Lamb. The day after He instituted this meal, He sacrificed Himself (see 42—44). He fulfilled the prophecy of John the Baptizer, who pointed to Jesus, saying, "Behold the Lamb of God who takes away the sin of the world." He offered a new meal to His disciples: His own body and blood.

In this Holy Supper Jesus gives His disciples His true body and true blood. They receive these blessings as they eat the bread and drink the wine of the Supper. This is the way that God binds Himself to us. Each Christian receives a personal promise for the forgiveness of all his sins when he partakes of this blessed meal. Jesus asks His disciples to eat this meal often. Every time they do, they remember His great sacrifice for all sinners.

When people partake of Jesus' Holy Supper, they make an important confession to other people. As they partake, it is as if they say aloud, "I am a condemned sinner. I have broken God's law. I truly accept forgiveness of all my sins because of Jesus' suffering and death." Only those who can make this kind of confession of their sins and their trust in Jesus should partake of this sacred meal. Only those who believe that they receive Jesus' true body and true blood in the sacrament should eat this meal together.

263

Jesus knew how much we need something earthly to understand His heavenly blessings. That's why He instituted His Holy Supper with bread and wine to eat and drink.

TO HELP US REMEMBER

Martin Luther's catechism contains the answers to the following questions: What is the Sacrament of the Altar? What is the benefit of such eating and drinking? How can bodily eating and drinking do such great things? Who then receives such Sacrament worthily? We want to remember his answers to these questions so that we may be better prepared to partake of this Holy Supper.

The words which Jesus used when He instituted this Holy Supper are found in Matthew 26, Mark 14, Luke 22, and 1 Corinthians 11. These are the words which the pastor speaks at the time of the celebration of the Holy Supper in church.

St. Paul summarizes Jesus' command to His disciples for all times:

> ✠ For as often as you eat this bread and drink the cup, you proclaim the Lord's death until He comes.
>
> *1 Corinthians 11:26*

WHAT THIS MEANS TO ME

I praise God for binding Himself to me in His Holy Supper! Jesus has given me something that I can *do* to show how close He is to me. As I eat the bread and drink the wine He gives me His body and blood. Even though I cannot understand, I do believe that in the Holy Supper, Jesus gives Himself to me.

When my congregation celebrates this Holy Supper, I join my fellow Christians as we confess our sins and look to Jesus for forgiveness. We believe that God will strengthen our faith through this Holy Supper and make us able to fight temptations to sin. I pray that every one who goes up to the Lord's Table will receive these heavenly blessings.

I look forward to my opportunity to take my place at the Lord's Table. At that time I can really praise God for binding Himself to me in His Holy Supper.

MY PRAYER

Lord Jesus, forgive my sins. Help me to be glad for every opportunity to receive Your true body and true blood in the Holy Supper. I praise You, with the Father and the Holy Spirit.

AMEN.

Jesus Christ, our blessed Savior,
Turned away God's wrath forever;
By His bitter grief and woe
He saved us from the evil Foe.

As His pledge of love undying
He, this precious food supplying,
Gives His body with the bread
And with the wine the blood He shed.

Praise the Father, who from heaven
Unto us such food hath given
And, to mend what we have done,
Gave into death His only Son.

The Lutheran Hymnal 311, st. 1, 2, 4

265

62

I PRAISE GOD

for making me His living epistle

This is the last chapter of the book. This book tells an amazing story—written in the Holy Scriptures and in the history of human beings. It is a story which began even before the beginning of time. It is a story which hasn't yet come to an end. There is still much more to come. Why is this the greatest story ever told to people? Because it tells about

GOD AT WORK

God started this whole world. He created life. All that He created was good. But God's creatures spoiled this goodness.

They disobeyed God, thinking that they could be as good as He was. God's creation was doomed to be eternally lost.

Then God made His plan of salvation for all men. He would redeem sinners and His whole creation. To put this plan of salvation into effect, God came into man's time. God chose certain people and spoke to them. He told them how He would place His special love upon them. He made a covenant with them to be their God and Lord; and He expected them to live as His covenant people. He told the world that His salvation for all men would come from these people.

When the time had fully come, God sent His Son into the world. Jesus was born of a human mother and placed under God's law. God became Man to be the Substitute for all sinners. This was the climax of God's plan of salvation. In Jesus Christ the plan came to a glorious conclusion. He kept the Law in the place of sinners. He suffered on the cross. He gave up His life as the supreme sacrifice. But He arose from the dead and lives today to protect and preserve His church which He founded before He left this world visibly at His ascension.

Why did God go to all this trouble and cost? He did this so that He could reconcile the world to Himself. He did all this so that we might be His people. St. Paul wrote, "Do you not know that your body is a temple of the Holy Spirit within you, which you have from God? You are not your own; you were bought with a price. So glorify God in your body" (1 Corinthians 6:19-20). We belong to God. We live to serve Him in everlasting righteousness and blessedness. How can we serve Him? By reflecting His love into the world from our own lives.

God has honored us by making us His living epistles. He wants people to know of His grace for all sinners as they read us in what we say and how we live. Some people may never get to read an epistle of St. Paul, but they may have the chance to see God at work in our way of life. God invites us to write a chapter in this greatest story ever told. His Holy Spirit gives us the power to be His disciples, showing His grace and love in Christ so that all men might be saved.

267

TO HELP US REMEMBER

We should remember the words of the apostle Paul as he describes this high honor which God gives us in making us His living epistles.

> ✠ You yourselves are our letter of recommendation, written on your hearts, to be known and read by all men; and you show that you are a letter from Christ delivered by us, written not with ink but with the Spirit of the living God, not on tablets of stone but on tablets of human hearts.
>
> *2 Corinthians 3:2-3*

Martin Luther's explanation to the *Second Article* of the Apostles' Creed is a familiar and stirring way of describing this relationship to God. We think of these words again as we look ahead to our part in the story of God's plan of salvation for sinners.

> I believe that Jesus Christ—true God, Son of the Father from eternity, and true man, born of the Virgin Mary—is my Lord. At great cost He has saved and redeemed me, a lost and condemned person. He has freed me from sin, death, and the power of the devil—not with silver or gold, but with His holy and precious blood and His innocent suffering and death. All this He has done that I may be His own, live under Him in His kingdom, and serve Him in everlasting righteousness, innocence, and blessedness, just as He is risen from the dead and lives and rules eternally. This is most certainly true.

WHAT THIS MEANS TO ME

I praise God for making me His living epistle. God saved me so that I might serve Him. God paid a high price so that He might redeem me. God promises me that I am His own to live under Him in His kingdom forever and ever. I can trust God never to break His promises.

I have an important work to do in my life. God expects people to read *His* love in the way in which *I* talk and act. That means that I use God's name as witness to my faith in Jesus — also in my prayers. I can speak kindly of other people. I want to help people rather than hurt them. I respect other people's property. I obey my parents and teachers. God made me His child. Everything I say and do is a part of the letter which people who know me are reading. His Spirit helps me witness to Jesus Christ.

It is a privilege to be God's letter which may strengthen my fellow Christians in their faith. I may even have the highest of all honors: be the letter by which God brings a new soul to salvation in Jesus Christ.

I praise God for giving noble purpose to my life.

MY PRAYER

> Almighty God, heavenly Father, I praise and thank
> You for redeeming me and making me Your child.
> I praise You for the honor of being a living letter
> of Your love for all sinners. By Your Holy Spirit
> help me to remember this high calling every day
> of my life. Give success to my efforts to witness to
> Your love and salvation in Jesus Christ.
>
> AMEN.

May we Thy precepts, Lord, fulfill
And do on earth our Father's will
As angels do above;
Still walk in Christ, the living Way,
With all Thy children and obey
The law of Christian love.

Spirit of Life, of Love, and Peace,
Unite our hearts, our joy increase,
Thy gracious help supply.
To each of us the blessing give
In Christian fellowship to live,
In joyful hope to die.

The Lutheran Hymnal 412, st. 1, 3

The Small Catechism

PART ONE

The Ten Commandments

I am the Lord your God.

THE FIRST COMMANDMENT

You shall have no other gods.

What does this mean for us?

We are to fear, love, and trust God above anything else.

THE SECOND COMMANDMENT

You shall not take the name of the Lord your God in vain.

What does this mean for us?

We are to fear and love God
so that we do not use His name superstitiously, or use it
to curse, swear, lie, or deceive,
but call on Him in prayer, praise, and thanksgiving.

THE THIRD COMMANDMENT

Remember the Sabbath Day, to keep it holy.

What does this mean for us?

We are to fear and love God
so that we do not neglect His Word and the preaching of it,
but regard it as holy
and gladly hear and learn it.

THE FOURTH COMMANDMENT

Honor your father and your mother.

What does this mean for us?

We are to fear and love God
so that we do not despise or anger our parents and others in authority,
but respect, obey, love, and serve them.

273

THE FIFTH COMMANDMENT

You shall not kill.

What does this mean for us?

We are to fear and love God
so that we do not hurt our neighbor in any way,
but help him in all his physical needs.

THE SIXTH COMMANDMENT

You shall not commit adultery.

What does this mean for us?

We are to fear and love God
so that in matters of sex our words and conduct are pure and
    honorable,
and husband and wife love and respect each other.

THE SEVENTH COMMANDMENT

You shall not steal.

What does this mean for us?

We are to fear and love God
so that we do not take our neighbor's money or property,
or get them in any dishonest way,
but help him to improve and protect
his property and means of making a living.

THE EIGHTH COMMANDMENT

You shall not bear false witness against your neighbor.

What does this mean for us?

We are to fear and love God
so that we do not betray, slander, or lie about our neighbor,
but defend him, speak well of him, and explain his actions in the
    kindest way.

THE NINTH COMMANDMENT

You shall not covet your neighbor's house.

What does this mean for us?

We are to fear and love God
so that we do not desire to get our neighbor's possessions by
  scheming,
or by pretending to have a right to them,
but always help him keep what is his.

THE TENTH COMMANDMENT

**You shall not covet your neighbor's wife or his man-
servant or his maidservant or his cattle or anything
that is your neighbor's.**

What does this mean for us?

We are to fear and love God
so that we do not tempt or coax away from our neighbor his wife
  or his workers,
but encourage them to remain loyal.

What does God say of all these commandments?

He says:
"I, the Lord your God, am a jealous God,
visiting the iniquity of the fathers upon the children to the third
  and fourth generation of those who hate Me,
but showing steadfast love to thousands of those who love Me and
  keep My commandments."

What does this mean for us?

God warns that He will punish all who break these commandments;
therefore we are to fear His wrath and not disobey Him.
But He promises grace and every blessing to all who keep these
  commandments;
therefore we are to love and trust Him, and gladly do what He
  commands.

PART TWO
The Apostles' Creed

THE FIRST ARTICLE

**I believe in God the Father Almighty,
Maker of heaven and earth.**

What does this mean?

I believe that God has created me and all that exists.

He has given me and still preserves
my body and soul with all their powers.

He provides me with food and clothing, home and family, daily work,
and all I need from day to day.

God also protects me in time of danger and guards me from every
evil.

All this He does out of fatherly and divine goodness and mercy,
though I do not deserve it.

Therefore I surely ought to thank and praise, serve and obey Him.

This is most certainly true.

THE SECOND ARTICLE

**And in Jesus Christ,
His only Son, our Lord;
who was conceived by the Holy Ghost,
born of the Virgin Mary;
suffered under Pontius Pilate,
was crucified, dead, and buried;
He descended into hell;
the third day He rose again from the dead;
He ascended into heaven,
and sitteth on the right hand of God the Father Almighty;
from thence He shall come to judge the quick and the
dead.**

What does this mean?

I believe that Jesus Christ—
true God, Son of the Father from eternity,
and true man, born of the Virgin Mary—
is my Lord.
At great cost He has saved and redeemed me, a lost and condemned
  person.
He has freed me from sin, death, and the power of the devil—
not with silver or gold,
but with His holy and precious blood
and His innocent suffering and death.
All this He has done that I may be His own,
live under Him in His kingdom,
and serve Him in everlasting righteousness, innocence, and blessedness,
just as He is risen from the dead and lives and rules eternally.
This is most certainly true.

THE THIRD ARTICLE

I believe in the Holy Ghost;
the holy Christian church, the communion of saints;
the forgiveness of sins;
the resurrection of the body;
and the life everlasting. Amen.

What does this mean?

I believe that I cannot by my own understanding or effort
believe in Jesus Christ, my Lord, or come to Him.
But the Holy Spirit has called me through the Gospel,
enlightened me with His gifts,
and sanctified and kept me in true faith.
In the same way He calls, gathers, enlightens, and sanctifies
the whole Christian church on earth,
and keeps it united with Jesus Christ in the one true faith.
In this Christian church day after day
He fully forgives my sins
and the sins of all believers.

On the last day He will raise me and all the dead
and give me and all believers in Christ eternal life.
This is most certainly true.

PART THREE

The Lord's Prayer

THE INTRODUCTION

Our Father who art in heaven.

What does this mean?

Here God encourages us to believe
that He is truly our Father
and we are His children.
We therefore are to pray to Him with complete confidence
just as children speak to their loving father.

THE FIRST PETITION

Hallowed be Thy name.

What does this mean?

God's name certainly is holy in itself,
but we ask in this prayer
that we may keep it holy.

When does this happen?

God's name is hallowed
whenever His Word is taught in its truth and purity
and we as children of God live in harmony with it.
Help us to do this, heavenly Father!

But anyone who teaches or lives contrary to the Word of God
dishonors God's name among us.
Keep us from doing this, heavenly Father!

THE SECOND PETITION

Thy kingdom come.

What does this mean?

God's kingdom comes indeed
without our praying for it,
but we ask in this prayer
that it may come also to us.

When does this happen?

God's kingdom comes
when our heavenly Father gives us His Holy Spirit,
so that by His grace we believe His holy Word
and live a godly life on earth now and in heaven forever.

THE THIRD PETITION

Thy will be done on earth as it is in heaven.

What does this mean?

The good and gracious will of God is surely done without our prayer,
but we ask in this prayer
that it may be done also among us.

When does this happen?

God's will is done when He hinders and defeats every evil scheme
     and purpose
of the devil, the world, and our sinful self,
which would prevent us from keeping His name holy
and would oppose the coming of His kingdom.
And His will is done
when He strengthens our faith
and keeps us firm in His Word as long as we live.
This is His gracious and good will.

THE FOURTH PETITION

Give us this day our daily bread.

What does this mean?

God gives daily bread, even without our prayer, to all people, though
    sinful,
but we ask in this prayer
that He will help us to realize this
and to receive our daily bread with thanks.

What is meant by "daily bread"?

Daily bread includes everything needed for this life,
such as food and clothing, home and property,
work and income, a devoted family,
an orderly community, good government,
favorable weather, peace and health,
a good name, and true friends and neighbors.

THE FIFTH PETITION

**And forgive us our trespasses,
As we forgive those who trespass against us.**

What does this mean?

We ask in this prayer
that our Father in heaven would not hold our sins against us
and because of them refuse to hear our prayer.
And we pray that He would give us everything by grace,
for we sin every day
and deserve nothing but punishment.
So we on our part will heartily forgive
and gladly do good to those who sin against us.

THE SIXTH PETITION

And lead us not into temptation.

What does this mean?

God tempts no one to sin,
but we ask in this prayer that God would watch over us and keep us
so that the devil, the world, and our sinful self may not deceive us
and draw us into false belief, despair, and other great and shameful
    sins.
And we pray that even though we are so tempted
we may still win the final victory.

THE SEVENTH PETITION

But deliver us from evil.

What does this mean?

We ask in this inclusive prayer
that our heavenly Father would save us from every evil to body and
    soul,
and at our last hour would mercifully take us
from the troubles of this world to·Himself in heaven.

THE DOXOLOGY

**For Thine is the kingdom
and the power and the glory
forever and ever.
Amen.**

What does "Amen" mean?

Amen means *Yes, it shall be so.*
We say *Amen* because we are certain
that such petitions are pleasing to our Father in heaven and are
    heard by Him.
For He Himself has commanded us to pray in this way
and has promised to hear us.

PART FOUR
The Sacrament of Holy Baptism

1

What is Baptism?

Baptism is not water only,
but it is water used together with God's Word and by His command.

What is this word?

In Matthew 28 our Lord Jesus Christ says:
"Go therefore and make disciples of all nations,
baptizing them in the name of the Father and of the Son and of the
    Holy Spirit."

2

What benefits does God give in Baptism?

In Baptism God forgives sin,
delivers from death and the devil,
and gives everlasting salvation to all who believe what He has promised.

What is God's promise?

In Mark 16 our Lord Jesus Christ says:
"He who believes and is baptized will be saved;
but he who does not believe will be condemned."

3

How can water do such great things?

It is not water that does these things,
but God's Word with the water and our trust in this Word.
Water by itself is only water,
but with the Word of God it is a life-giving water
which by grace gives the new birth through the Holy Spirit.
St. Paul writes in Titus 3:
"He saved us . . . in virtue of His own mercy,
by the washing of regeneration and renewal in the Holy Spirit,

which He poured out upon us richly
through Jesus Christ our Savior,
so that we might be justified by His grace
and become heirs in hope of eternal life.
The saying is sure."

4

What does Baptism mean for daily living?

It means that our sinful self, with all its evil deeds and desires,
should be drowned through daily repentance;
and that day after day a new self should arise
to live with God in righteousness and purity forever.
St. Paul writes in Romans 6:
"We were buried therefore with Him by Baptism into death,
so that as Christ was raised from the dead by the glory of the Father,
we too might walk in newness of life."

PART FIVE

The Sacrament of Holy Communion

1

What is Holy Communion?

Holy Communion is the body and blood of
our Lord Jesus Christ given with bread
and wine, instituted by Christ Himself
for us to eat and drink.

Where do the Scriptures say this?

Matthew, Mark, Luke, and Paul say:
Our Lord Jesus Christ, in the night in which He was betrayed,
took bread; and when He had given thanks,
He broke it and gave it to His disciples,
saying, "Take, eat; this is My body, which is given for you;
this do in remembrance of Me."

After the same manner also He took the cup after supper,
and when He had given thanks,
He gave it to them, saying,
"Drink of it, all of you;
this cup is the new testament in My blood,
which is shed for you and for many for the remission of sins;
this do, as often as you drink it, in remembrance of Me."

2

What benefits do we receive from this sacrament?

The benefits of this sacrament are pointed out by the words,
given and shed for you for the remission of sins.
These words assure us that in the sacrament
we receive forgiveness of sins, life, and salvation.
For where there is forgiveness of sins,
there is also life and salvation.

3

How can eating and drinking do all this?

It is not eating and drinking that does this,
but the words, *given and shed for you for the remission of sins.*
These words, along with eating and drinking, are the main thing in
the sacrament.
And whoever believes these words
has exactly what they say, forgiveness of sins.

4

When is a person rightly prepared to receive this sacrament?

Fasting and other outward preparations serve a good purpose.
However, that person is well prepared and worthy who believes these
words,
given and shed for you for the remission of sins.
But anyone who does not believe these words, or doubts them,
is neither prepared nor worthy,
for the words *for you* require simply a believing heart.

PART SIX

The Office of the Keys

What is the "Office of the Keys"?

It is that authority which Christ gave to His church
to forgive the sins of those who repent
and to declare to those who do not repent
that their sins are not forgiven.

What are the words of Christ?

Our Lord Jesus Christ said to His disciples:
"Receive the Holy Spirit. If you forgive the sins of
any, they are forgiven; if you retain the sins of any,
they are retained." (John 20:23)

"Truly, I say to you, Whatever you bind on earth shall
be bound in heaven, and whatever you loose on earth
shall be loosed in heaven." (Matthew 18:18)

Confession

What is private confession?

Private confession has two parts. First, we make a personal confession of sins to the pastor, and then we receive absolution,
which means forgiveness as from God Himself. This absolution
we should not doubt, but firmly believe that thereby our sins are
forgiven before God in heaven.

What sins should we confess?

Before God we should confess that we are guilty of all sins, even
those which are not known to us, as we do in the Lord's Prayer.
But in private confession, as before the pastor, we should confess only those sins which trouble us in heart and mind.

What are such sins?

We can examine our everyday life according to the Ten Commandments—for example, how we act toward father or mother, son or daughter, husband or wife, or toward the people with whom we work, and so on. We may ask ourselves whether we have been disobedient or unfaithful, bad-tempered or dishonest, or whether we have hurt anyone by word or deed.

How might we confess our sins privately?

We may say that we wish to confess our sins and to receive absolution in God's name. We may begin by saying, "I, a poor sinner, confess before God that I am guilty of many sins." Then we should name the sins that trouble us. We may close the confession with the words, "I repent of all these sins and pray for mercy. I promise to do better with God's help."

What if we are not troubled by any special sins?

We should not torture ourselves with imaginary sins. If we cannot think of any sins to confess (which would hardly ever happen), we need not name any in particular, but may receive absolution because we have already made a general confession to God.

How may we be assured of forgiveness?

The pastor may pronounce the absolution by saying, "By the authority of our Lord Jesus Christ I forgive you your sins in the name of the Father and of the Son and of the Holy Spirit. Amen."

Those who are heavily burdened in conscience the pastor may comfort and encourage with further assurances from God's Word.

Prayers

MORNING PRAYER

In the morning when you get up, make the sign of the holy cross and say:

In the name of ✠ the Father and of the Son and of the Holy Ghost. Amen.

Then, kneeling or standing, repeat the Creed and the Lord's
Prayer. If you choose you may also say this little prayer:

I thank Thee, my heavenly Father,
through Jesus Christ, Thy dear Son,
that Thou hast kept me this night from all harm and danger;
and I pray Thee that Thou wouldst keep me this day also
from sin and every evil,
that all my doings and life may please Thee.
For into Thy hands I commend myself,
my body and soul, and all things,
Let Thy holy angel be with me
that the wicked Foe may have no power over me. Amen.

After singing a hymn (possibly a hymn on the Ten Commandments)
or whatever your devotion may suggest, you should go to your work
joyfully.

EVENING PRAYER

In the evening when you go to bed, make the sign of the holy
cross and say:

In the name of ✠ the Father and of the Son and of the Holy
    Ghost. Amen.

Then, kneeling or standing, repeat the Creed and the Lord's
Prayer. If you choose you may also say this little prayer:

I thank Thee, my heavenly Father,
through Jesus Christ, Thy dear Son,
that Thou hast graciously kept me this day;
and I pray Thee that Thou wouldst forgive me all my sins
    where I have done wrong
and graciously keep me this night.
For into Thy hands I commend myself,
my body and soul, and all things.
Let Thy holy angel be with me
that the wicked Foe may have no power over me. Amen.

Then go to sleep at once and in good cheer.

BLESSING BEFORE EATING

When children and the whole household gather at the table, they
should reverently fold their hands and say:

The eyes of all look to Thee, O Lord,
and Thou givest them their food in due season.
Thou openest Thy hand; Thou satisfiest the desire of every
      living thing.

Then the Lord's Prayer should be said and afterwards this
prayer:
Lord God, heavenly Father, bless us
and these Thy gifts which we receive from Thy bountiful goodness,
through Jesus Christ our Lord. Amen.

THANKSGIVING AFTER EATING

Likewise after eating they should fold their hands
reverently and say:
O give thanks to the Lord, for He is good,
for His steadfast love endures forever.
He gives to the beasts their food and to the young ravens
      which cry.
His delight is not in the strength of the horse, nor His
      pleasure in the legs of a man;
but the Lord takes pleasure in those who fear Him, in those
      who hope in His steadfast love.

Then the Lord's Prayer should be said and afterwards this prayer:
We give Thee thanks, Lord God, our Father, for all Thy benefits,
through Jesus Christ our Lord, who lives and reigns forever. Amen.